"Many church planters are burdened by a limited view of success. We often measure our work and our worth by what can be immediately tallied—bodies, bucks, and buildings. In *Rethinking the Successful Church*, Dr. Rima provides a larger and more accurate measuring stick."

—Dave Reynolds, director
Northwest Church Planting

"*Rethinking the Successful Church* offers constructive criticism of current reliance upon formula-mediated methodologies, processes, and approaches to building 'successful' churches. Sam's refreshing approach brings God back into the center of ministry activity where he belongs."

—Greg Bourgond, D.Min., Ed.D., vice president
Operations & Strategic Initiatives
Bethel Theological Seminary

"This book should be required reading for seminary students, elders, pastors, and ministry leaders of all kinds. Sam speaks from personal experience, challenging us to think carefully about our motivations in ministry. He delivers a timely reminder of how God often measures success quite differently than we do. Read the book, be encouraged by its message, and trust that God knows what's best for you and your ministry!"

—Cheri Keaggy, recording artist

"Balance is the key to a healthy ministry. Dr. Rima shouts with passion and reason for a return to balance in our expectations of what the church should be under God's leadership."

—Jan D. Hettinga, senior pastor
Northshore Baptist Church
Snohomish, Washington

D0369447

After serving as a local church pastor for seventeen years, Sam Rima now serves as the District Executive Minister of the Columbia Baptist Conference. The Columbia Baptist Conference consists of all of the Baptist General Conference churches in the states of Alaska, Washington, Oregon, Idaho, and Montana. Sam serves as adjunct faculty at Bethel Seminary and North American Baptist Seminary and has also taught at Talbot School of Theology, Biola University, and Grace University in Omaha, Nebraska. Sam also leads many workshops and seminars annually on the subjects of leadership and spiritual formation. Sam lives on Puget Sound in Washington State with his wife of twenty years, Sue, and their four children, Jill, Seth, Hillary, and Sammy.

For information about workshops or classes, contact Dr. Sam Rima at samrima2@aol.com or at:

The Columbia Baptist Conference
925 North 130th Street
Seattle, WA 98133
206-365-9890

RETHINKING THE *Successful* CHURCH

Finding Serenity in God's Sovereignty

Samuel D. Rima

Brad –
So glad God brought us together! I think of
you often and pray for God's best in your life.
Stay close to Him and he will use you
greatly! Congrats!   Sam
                              3/2/02

BakerBooks

A Division of Baker Book House Co
Grand Rapids, Michigan 49516

Other books by Samuel Rima

Leading from the Inside Out
Overcoming the Dark Side of Leadership (with Gary L. McIntosh)

© 2002 by Samuel D. Rima

Published by Baker Books
a division of Baker Book House Company
P.O. Box 6287, Grand Rapids, MI 49516-6287

Printed in the United States of America

Library of Congress Cataloging-in-Publication Data

Rima, Samuel D.
    Rethinking the successful church : finding serenity in God's sovereignty / Samuel D. Rima.
        p.   cm.
    Includes bibliographical references (p.).
    ISBN 0-8010-9117-9 (paper)
    1. Pastoral theology—Baptists. I. Title.
    BV4011.3 .R56   2001
    253—dc21   2001052723

For current information about all releases from Baker Book House, visit our web site:

                            http://www.bakerbooks.com

Contents

To

My physical parents, Stan and Phyllis Rima, who gave me physical life and who have shown me what true success really looks like

And to

My spiritual parents, the Rev. Robert L. Griffin and his wife, Ramona, whom God used to give me spiritual life and who have shown me what success in ministry really looks like

Acknowledgments

If this book is of value to any reader, it is because of God's grace and his patience in using a vessel like me. The content of this book is the result of lessons learned on the potter's wheel, at times painful and frightening but always needed. It is truly a mystery to me why God has chosen to place his eternal treasure of the gospel and its result of salvation in such frail earthen pots. But I am nevertheless eternally grateful!

Additionally, as with my previous books, I owe a debt of gratitude to my wife, Sue, who is a constant source of encouragement and one of God's greatest gifts to me in this life. God continues to teach me about himself through her.

Leighton Ford has been a source of untold wisdom and direction for me during this season of my life and a true friend on the journey. He has facilitated my ability to hear the voice of God on more than one occasion ask, "What is the seed that must die?" Thanks for letting God ask me that question through you, Leighton.

To the staff and Elder Board at Central Baptist Church, thanks so much for allowing me and encouraging me to follow the call of God on my life. My time serving with you has been one of the highlights of my life.

And to Mary Suggs who once again provided her editorial expertise to this manuscript, making it more coherent and readable than I ever could. Mary, thanks for your inquisitive mind and your ability to ask the probing questions that have made this a better book.

Introduction

Like many in ministry, I have struggled with what it means to be successful as a pastor called to full-time Christian service. In my quest for ministry success I have followed many formulas, attended countless seminars, purchased ministry tool kits galore, and read more than my fair share of how-to books. And yet, in spite of my search for the secrets of ministry success, the success I originally sought has eluded me. Many of my attempts to "be successful" left me feeling more miserable and frustrated than they did fulfilled. It wasn't long before I began questioning the nature of true success in ministry. At some point I began to realize that maybe what I had been pursuing for so many years didn't even exist. Like the heat mirage on a hot summer road, every time I reached a place in my ministry journey where I thought I would experience "success" and the serenity and contentment I knew should accompany such an achievement, I still felt the same—restless and desperate. So began my odyssey of "rethinking the successful church."

The purpose of this book is to help ministry leaders rediscover the joy and serenity of serving God by being fully aware of his sovereignty over the ministry process. When our church is driven by a clear purpose and has a concise statement of mission as well as a compelling vision, we can recognize a measure of success and find serenity in acknowledging and then accepting God's sovereignty, even if we do not see the results we anticipated.

At the same time, this book is not endorsing sloppy, unfocused, lazy ministry, with the excuse of letting God be God. But rather it is a call to excellence in ministry that always bears in mind that God has authority over our planning and programs, not merely as a form of spiritual or theological tokenism but in sober recognition of the transcendent, cosmic reality that God is indeed sovereign over and in his church.

My prayer is that God will use this book to facilitate the beginning of a journey back to joy in ministry for those who, in search of ministry success, have been unwittingly entranced and obsessed with the megachurch amulet.

As you read, allow the journey toward finding serenity in God's sovereignty and joy in ministry begin for you.

ONE

Megachurch Mania

Our Obsession with Ministry Success

Since the early 1980s, those being trained for pastoral ministry, as well as those already leading in the local church setting, have had an almost manic obsession with the megachurch.

Though primarily a phenomenon of the last two decades, the megachurch (that is, churches with average worship attendance of 1,500 or more) has become the standard by which many, if not most, pastors and lay church leaders measure their ministry success or, conversely, their lack of success.

Having come of age as a minister during this period of time, I know this obsession well, and I believe I have plenty of company. Of concern to me is that we pastors who have come of age during the rise of the megachurch movement are now plagued in large measure by a pervasive obsession with it.

Not many pastors would willingly or readily admit that they are obsessed with developing the next Willow Creek or Saddleback Community Church. However, if hooked up to a polygraph and asked if they would be satisfied and content if their church never experienced substantial growth, most pastors would have to answer no or risk the needle of said polygraph jumping off the page in seismic gyrations, indicating that a significant untruth had been told.

Though most ministers could quickly and convincingly justify their obsession as a genuine desire to reach the world for Christ and expand the kingdom of God, the stark reality is that much of what fuels this obsession is actually a desperate desire and need to succeed in one's chosen field of endeavor, thus providing a measure of self-validation.

Learning the Megachurch Mantra

Has this obsession with church growth and the megachurch been something that has historically captured the hearts of the clergy? Or is this actually a relatively new emphasis within the ranks of the ordained? Paradoxically, the answer is probably both yes and no.

Like all people who aspire to positions of leadership, those who enter ministry bring with them their own dark-side issues that drive them to achieve whatever it is they have determined success to be for them. For some that may involve the attainment of a certain level of proficiency in the area of public proclamation. Still others may define success as earning an advanced graduate degree or having a book published. The definition of success is different for every church leader. And yet, though success is defined differently for virtually every leader, when it comes to those who are practitioners in the local church, particularly those of a more evangelical stripe, the phenomenon that seems to almost universally be seen as a sign of success is church growth.

12

And not just any growth will suffice. Success to most local church pastors and those who monitor them requires substantial numerical growth that is obviously noticeable to others—both those inside and outside the church. Try as we might to subdue the megachurch monster of success that constantly seems to stalk us as church leaders, it always seems to leap on us at the most unexpected and unwanted times.

However, we are not entirely to blame for our fixation with church growth and the "bigger is better" syndrome. The seminaries we have attended and the seminars in which we have been encouraged to participate have fed this obsession. In fact, when evangelical seminaries and denominations utilize the pastors of these churches as keynote speakers and guest lecturers to the exclusion of pastors of lesser renown, they subtly imply that the famous megachurches are the ecclesiastical benchmark by which all churches should be measured.

At this point, I can imagine many of you rolling your eyes and mustering a compelling rebuttal against what must appear to the reasonable reader to be an anti–church-growth philosophy of ministry that maligns the megachurch and those who lead it. However, nothing could be further from the truth.

First of all, let me say that I am unequivocally in favor of church growth. In fact I was the senior pastor of a church of one thousand and I still hope and pray that that already sizable and healthy ministry will continue to see growth. You can believe me when I say that I am in favor of the megachurch. Additionally, I firmly believe that the emergence of the megachurch on the twentieth-century church landscape has introduced more positive benefits to American evangelicalism than it has negative effects from any abuses or distortions precipitated by overzealous proponents of this model.

I have visited many of today's megachurches, which have become tantamount to Mecca for pastors and church planters. I have gained invaluable insights and principles from these churches and their leaders, which have led to more effective ministry in my own exercise of church leadership. I am all in favor of the leadership conferences and seminars for creative ministry, hosted by today's megachurches, and heartily endorse the benefits of these conferences to any pastor.

So, what's my problem? Now that I have successfully spoken out of both sides of my mouth, what is the purpose and point of this book?

From Mania to Middle Ground

What I am arguing for is a rejection of our heretofore manic obsession with the megachurch in favor of a perspective that might possibly promote a more healthy middle ground from which ministers and church leaders might pursue a more physically, emotionally, and spiritually balanced ministry and actually enjoy the journey in the process.

The term *mania* describes an irrational excitement or enthusiasm for, or an uncontrolled focus on, something. We get our word *maniac* from this word. When we say that an individual is a maniac we are saying that he or she is irrationally consumed by an enthusiasm or obsession for something.

I love to hunt upland game birds. There are few things I enjoy more than lazily trailing behind my dog, Ginger, on a crisp fall day in pursuit of ringneck pheasants, quail, woodcock, or any other legitimate game bird. Closer to the truth, most who know me well would be quick to say that my love of hunting is more of an obsession than it is a casual interest. When the hunting season rolls around, I want to be in the field every possible opportunity that I get. Testifying to my obsession are the times I have unintentionally put my life in jeopardy by attempting to hunt in dangerously inclement weather. Even with a 20-mile-per-hour wind and a wind chill of 60 below zero, I have been known to trudge through knee-deep snow in an effort to bag a few birds.

Now, to the casual observer (or should I say the sane observer), such behavior makes little sense. How can such a miserable activity be fun? The only reasonable answer is that I am a hunting maniac. I have an irrational obsession with this sport that few others can understand. Though it often results in physical pain and misery and on one occasion a near deadly accident in my truck, I still enjoy hunting. And at times, the more difficult the conditions, the more I enjoy the hunt.

Similarly, it would be safe to say that in the last twenty years many ministers have become megachurch maniacs. For these pastors, church size and growth have become the all-consuming objects of their excitement and enthusiasm. In spite of the fact that this obsession has led to a tremendous increase in the number of pastoral failures and episodes of burnout, many ministers still insist on stalking the elusive megachurch. Though for many clergy this obsession with growth has sucked the joy and fulfillment out of their ministry, many still are compelled to risk it all and sacrifice their enjoyment of pastoral ministry in favor of bagging the big church. Surely this qualifies as maniacal behavior!

The costs to the church of such an irrational obsession have been heavy. The most frequent casualty of our obsession with growth has been the generation of believers who built most of our churches during the decades following the Second World War. Since the members of this "Builder" generation, as they have been labeled, may be uncomfortable with the megachurch model and

15

cannot make much sense of this pastoral obsession with bigger-is-better, they have often found themselves programmed out or planned around as the church staff maintains its course toward megachurch status. These older parishioners frequently become nothing more than irritating roadblocks to the great church we want to build, and subconsciously we may label them "traditionalists" or "complainers," who threaten to block our dream. Surely this is not a healthy state of affairs in the church of Jesus Christ.

Other casualties have been in the area of congregational and individual spiritual formation. For many churches that have attained the status of a megachurch the concern I most often hear from their pastors is, "We've become a mile wide and an inch deep." Such rapid growth does not easily lend itself to the establishment and fostering of the intimate sense of community so essential to the healthy and holistic spiritual formation of believers.

Still other churches that have aspired to large-church status have found themselves severely overextended financially, even to the point that their debt significantly threatens their continued existence.

What I am trying to say is that when our sole focus is on growth and reaching a certain numerical goal, to the exclusion of other equally vital signs of ministry, megachurch mania becomes more destructive than productive. It becomes destructive to pastors as they place themselves under tremendous pressure to perform in a way that will produce substantial growth. It can become destructive to parishioners, as their spiritual leaders always seem to be looking just beyond them to the needs of those not yet assimilated into the church. It becomes destructive to those established churches that vainly struggle to become something that very possibly God never intended them to be. This obsession can become destructive to the very mission of growth that we espouse as we begin to use people as a means to the end of church growth, rather than seeing the growth and spiritual development of these people as the more desirable end that will then provide more balanced and healthy church growth.

Mega Misery

So why is it, in the face of such detrimental potential results, that many pastors and church leaders continue to obsessively pursue the megachurch course? It seems to me that many in pastoral ministry today are looking to derive their personal happiness and sense of worth as a person from their success in ministry. Though this is generally not easily admitted by ministry professionals, the reality is, albeit subconscious for many leaders, that their sense of personal value, worth, and even identity is dependent on their achievement of success in their ministry. And, as we have seen, success today is most often equated with growth, significant growth.

As a result, many pastors are driven by the belief that their sense of fulfillment and worth as a person lurks just beyond the next growth barrier. If they could just lead their congregation through that ominous 400 barrier, then they would find the sense of worth and fulfillment they seek. However, as they near the horizon to 400, the sense of serenity and inner worth they had hoped to find is still mysteriously missing. Maybe it is out there beyond 800 or 1,000. And so the megachurch monster continues to be fed, lunching on yet another pastor's joy and satisfaction in ministry.

You see, when we allow ourselves to become obsessed with church growth, like any unhealthy addiction, we soon develop a tolerance for what once produced a sense

17

of satisfaction. Then we need to up our dosage from 400 to 800, then 800 to 1,000; and so the miserable obsession goes on.

I personally experienced the misery of megachurch mania when I fell under its intoxicating influence during the late 1980s while serving as a church planter in southern California. In all honesty, I began my church-planting effort with nothing but the most spiritually altruistic intentions. I did not set out intending to build the next Crystal Cathedral or Willow Creek. My sole desire was, by God's grace, to establish a foothold for the kingdom amid the rapidly growing area of southern California to which I had been assigned. I truly wanted to develop in that place a solid, spiritually healthy group of genuine believers.

But strangely, almost imperceptibly, my motives and desires began to subtly shift. As our little church began to grow, even beyond my expectations, my initial standards for ministry success were no longer sufficient. Without warning I began thinking *Hey, there's no telling how far I might be able to take this thing!*

At first I was satisfied with mere survival, but then growth and success created within me an appetite for more growth, which I would soon discover could not be easily satisfied. Insidiously, methodology and marketing to produce growth began to take priority over prayer and an absolute reliance on the Holy Spirit of God. I began to covet the numerical growth of other churches and firmly believed that if they could do it, then so could I. I began to believe that if only I did the right things, applied the proper techniques, and raised enough money, I could simply manufacture church growth, just like a mortgage banker increases his or her market share. I was experiencing the onset of full-blown megachurch mania and I was growing increasingly miserable in ministry.

My obsession with church growth also produced within me a decidedly competitive spirit. It was becoming increasingly difficult, if not altogether impossible, to rejoice with the published successes of other churches. Instead of sharing in their success as a fellow kingdom-builder and rejoicing in what God was doing, I silently chalked up their growth to dumb luck or the possibility that they were the benefactors of more advantageous circumstances than I was. When denominational leaders bragged about what God was doing in a sister congregation, I jealously wished that the object of their praise were my growing congregation and me.

Now, I always went through the motions of being excited for the growth God was producing in other congregations. But beneath my spiritual facade I was jealous of their success and would silently determine to redouble my efforts to produce the growth I had begun to believe was my divine right, as well as the probable solution to my search for a sense of spiritual serenity, professional success, and personal validation.

These are some of the symptoms of megachurch mania we church leaders may become aware of if we allow God to get our attention for a moment. When we are experiencing misery and a manic drivenness in ministry, we must be quick to see the warning lights flashing on the dashboard of our life. This is not what God intends for those in his service. Though ministry is demanding and at times very stressful to be sure, amid the stress and demands there should be a certain measure of inner serenity and even joy.

Am I suggesting that ministry should always be enjoyable and trouble-free? Do I naively believe that as pastors we will never experience the pain of gospel ministry that is a natural by-product of our engaging the adversary on the front lines? Absolutely not! I've been in ministry too long and done battle with enough well-

19

intentioned dragons to know better. But I have also personally experienced the frantic, manic ministry life that my own dark side and fragile personal ego needs have produced, and I want to warn others in ministry of the dangers of improperly trying to satisfy those needs.

A Common Story

During the last fifteen years, as the megachurch has made its way to the covers of *Time* and *Newsweek* and has been profiled on major television networks, Dean's story has become more common than we would care to admit.

Dean came out of seminary in the late '80s with the "can-do" attitude and "take no prisoners" philosophy of a freshly shaved marine recruit who firmly believed he was one of God's "few good men" who would take it to the enemy as a well-equipped, heavily armed church planter.

Dean never even questioned whether or not his church would experience rapid growth; he simply assumed that church-growth success was his for the taking. After all, how could growth allude him, armed as he was with telemarketing programs that virtually guaranteed an opening Sunday of 200-plus parishioners, direct mailing plans that promised up to a 1 percent positive return, and proven principles that would propel him through those early, irritating little growth barriers. Based on his DISC profile and "ENTJ" Myers-Briggs profile tests, he was a tailor-made church planter; "a sure success," those who should know told him.

Well, Dean did see some exciting church growth. His church plant took off and rapidly developed a solid core group. His church immediately blew through the 200 barrier and was soon pulsating with a spiritual life and

20

vitality that caused it to begin pressing up against the 400 barrier. But somewhere around 400 Dean's church stalled out. For a little over a year there was no significant growth. Dean's solution? One more mass mailing campaign promoting a new community event should do the trick. But Dean's church could not muster the energy to pull it off with the fervor and commitment he had come to expect from his fledgling group of innovative Boomers and Busters. After four years of one growth program being conducted closely on the heels of another, and a church infrastructure that could barely sustain the current attendance, the new congregation was beginning to stabilize a bit.

Of course, this began to frustrate and anger Dean. "Don't they know there are people going to hell out there?" With each month of relative stability Dean grew increasingly impatient and miserable. After four years of success, he felt as though he was beginning to see his dreams of nonstop growth threatened. Dean began to question his leadership style and ministry methods. Surely there had to be a solution to get the church back into growth mode.

As each new attempt at manufacturing growth resulted in little more than a temporary buzz of activity, Dean grew increasingly introspective and frustrated. Not long after the church began to stabilize at 400, Dean's frustration with the church spilled over into his marriage. His wife, Mary, had felt like a third wheel for quite some time, and now they were experiencing difficulties they never imagined could happen to them.

Finally, after five years of what most would consider a highly successful ministry, Dean left his church. With a sense of personal defeat and discouragement, he moved on, looking for the next challenge that might provide the opportunity for him to realize his dream of being a megachurch pastor.

Process Not Product

Again let me clearly state that I am not against church growth—I am all for it! I do not believe the megachurch is "McChurch" as some have sarcastically labeled it. I am convinced that the Willow Creeks and Saddlebacks are a wonderful work of God. I am not bashing church growth or church-growth technology. In fact I am very active in the church-growth efforts of our denomination and have been the chairman of my previous district's Church Planting Committee, encompassing the states of North Dakota, South Dakota, Nebraska, Kansas, and Missouri. I long to see more growing churches planted and already established churches revitalized. But what I am concerned about is our tendency to reduce the church of God, the mystical body of Christ, to a mere product that can be manufactured by our own efforts while neglecting the process God uses to expand his universal church. When we reduce ministry to a product rather than an experience in which God is the sovereign, we miss out on the joy and deep sense of spiritual satisfaction that can come from simply being a small part of God's process.

Finding Serenity in God's Sovereignty

What I am advocating in this book is that we in the church-growth movement refocus on God's sovereignty in this amazing process. I am suggesting that we can experience a certain degree of serenity in our ministry efforts when we again recognize the role God's sovereignty plays in the process of church growth.

Even when our church stabilizes for a period of time, in spite of our best efforts at growth, and we're not seeing the level of growth we might desire or even expect, we need to recognize that it is God's church not ours. We need to be reminded that God grows his church for his own glory and not to satisfy our neurotic ego needs. God is not on a five-year growth plan when it comes to his church. He has a unique purpose and plan for each of his local manifestations of his universal body, and our role as leaders in this church is to discover his purpose and then facilitate his plan.

When that begins to take place, it removes a tremendous burden from our ministry shoulders that we were never intended to carry and we can begin to enjoy the process of ministry once again or, very possibly, begin enjoying it for the first time.

Suggestions for Self-Reflection

1. Take some time to reflect on the ministry practitioners you look to as models or leaders you admire. Being as honest as possible, on what have you based your admiration? What role has their success in ministry played in their becoming models for you?
2. Take some time right now to reflect on how obsessed you have been with the growth (or lack of growth) of the church(es) you have served in the last ten years.
3. What reasons can you give for your obsession with church growth—why is it so important to you?
4. Can you relate with Dean's story on pages 20–21? In what ways?
5. Do you see church growth more as a process or a product? Explain.
6. At the present time, how content are you in your current ministry?

23

7. If you are content in your current ministry, what reasons would you give for your contentment? Is your contentment connected to what appears to be a "successful" ministry?

8. If you are not content at the present time, what would need to change for you to begin experiencing a renewed sense of contentment?

9. Could you be content if your church or ministry endeavor never experienced significant growth? Why or why not?

TWO

Recipes for Success

Just Follow the Formula

Everyone has a favorite recipe. Mine happens to be my mother's recipe for yeast cinnamon rolls. One of the reasons it has become my favorite recipe is that over the course of many years it has remained the same—I can count on delicious rolls every time my mother uses it.

Regardless of the location in which my mother happens to be making those cinnamon rolls and in spite of changing equipment and passing time, the one thing I can count on is that if my mother, or anyone else for that matter, follows that recipe precisely, the end result will be the same. Following that recipe will always yield delicious, mouth-watering cinnamon rolls that rival even Cinnabon!

A favorite recipe becomes a favorite because it works! Regardless of who throws the ingredients together and in spite of where those ingredients are thrown together, if the recipe is closely followed, the final product will always be the same. Recipes are kind of nice in that regard. That's why it is possible to sell cookbooks, because people have confidence in the concept of following a recipe, knowing that it will produce a specific result or product.

Instant Formulas

The reality is that recipes are not just for food. There are recipes for virtually everything imaginable today. All you have to do is turn on the television to be bombarded by countless recipes or formulas that promise to produce a specific, desirable result. There are people like Anthony Robbins, who promises personal power and unlimited success if you purchase his "recipe book" and diligently follow the formula that is provided. It worked for him. So it will work for you—just follow the formula!

Actress turned fitness guru Suzanne Somers hawks the TorsoTrac abdominal workout machine, guaranteeing that if you purchase this piece of "special" equipment and follow the formula laid out in the video provided, you too will possess washboard abs.

Don Lapre has developed and refined a recipe for making loads of money by placing tiny little advertisements in a lot of newspapers. He has developed his formula to such a degree that he promises anyone who buys his "recipe book" to see the same result that he and countless other followers of the formula have produced. I think you get the picture!

Today we are a culture awash in instant formulas for success. It seems that we as people so desperately want to see positive and productive things take place in our lives that we convince ourselves there truly are legitimate formulas for success out there—formulas that will work for anyone—we just have to find them and then faithfully follow them!

26

Could it be that this same mentality has found its way into the church and has begun to influence Christian leaders in their practice of ministry? Is it at all possible that a significant percentage of American pastors and spiritual leaders have unwittingly succumbed to this mentality, believing that with the right formula they can produce the very desirable result of church growth? Unfortunately, I am afraid the answer is yes.

A Recipe for Ministry Success

Curt, a young pastor I know, attended a special seminar that promised to help him unlock the secret to producing significant church growth. He paid his registration fee, traveled to a distant city, checked into his hotel room, and then anxiously waited for the seminar to begin the next morning. Curt went prepared to learn. He was committed to do whatever it might take to see his church grow and reach more people for Christ. He felt confident that this seminar was just what he needed because the church of the pastor presenting the material had experienced exponential growth by implementing the very same principles he was going to be sharing with the seminar attendees. If it worked for his church, Curt reasoned, it had to work for other churches.

Curt was incredibly attentive to the successful pastor as he spoke, and he conscientiously recorded even the most seemingly insignificant insights that were shared. In spite of his studious and focused engagement during the sessions, Curt was worried that he might somehow miss a crucial step or element of the strategy being shared. Luckily for him, the resource table at the seminar displayed a tool kit that could be purchased, which provided a step-by-step process for

27

implementing the principles of the seminar in a way that was virtually fail-safe.

So, with more than just a little excitement, Curt picked up one of the tool kits and could hardly wait to get home to his church so that he could begin following the formula for church growth he had just learned.

As he flew home, Curt broke out the tool kit and began devouring it at 36,000 feet. According to the tool kit, the first course of action that needed to be taken (if he wanted the program to work) was to convene a meeting of his board members and, using the overheads provided, lay out the program for them so that they could see the exciting things that were in store for their church. Once that meeting had been conducted, they could begin to implement the plan in earnest.

On arriving home Curt wasted no time in writing a letter to his board members informing them of the "planning" meeting that was being scheduled. In reality it wasn't going to be a planning meeting as much as it was going to be an information meeting, as Curt had already determined the course of action that they were going to follow. What he really wanted was for his board members to enthusiastically endorse and embrace this exciting new strategy that would produce significant growth for their church.

Unfortunately, the board was not quite as enthusiastic as their young pastor was. Several of the board members bristled at the pastor's well-intentioned attempt to get approval for the program after a single meeting. Several elders suggested that maybe they should take a few weeks to study the program and make a determination on whether or not to implement it, based on its merits and how much it was going to cost.

But in spite of the resistance Curt was able to gain approval, though it was less than the enthusiastic endorsement for which he had hoped, and he determined to move ahead immediately—which he did.

After nearly three months of planning and another three months of implementation, Curt and the congregation anxiously awaited the Celebration Sunday that was to be the culmination of all their hard work. They had followed the plan carefully and had no reason to expect anything but total success. As a result of their calling, mailings, radio advertising, and the exciting program they had planned and promoted for the event, they had good reason to approach Celebration Sunday with high hopes. This would be the Sunday they would turn the corner and finally break the 200 barrier that had been holding them back from more significant growth.

On Celebration Sunday there was an almost palpable sense of excitement among members of the congregation as they waited for guests to flood the parking lot. But the anticipated flood was actually more like a trickle as unfamiliar faces only sporadically entered the building. When the final attendance tally was made, the number was more than just a little disappointing. There had been fewer that twenty guests who could be considered legitimate, first-time, nonchurched visitors, not nearly the number that had been expected or promised by the seminar speaker and the tool kit. It was a significant disappointment for those who had poured so much of their time and energy into the program over the past six months—not to mention the substantial amount of money that had been given to fund it.

In the weeks and months that followed Celebration Sunday, Curt found himself slogging through an emotional and spiritual slump that was sapping his energy and enthusiasm for ministry. Exacerbating his emotional pain was the fact that the elders who initially resisted immediate implementation and had suggested more time to study the program were expressing their disappointment and concern with the outcome of the program. It had not been a positive experience for my friend or his church. They had failed. The formula that had worked for so many others had not worked for them.

In the wake of this perceived failure, Curt began to question his giftedness for pastoral ministry and felt that he had lost credibility with some of his elders. He had expended a healthy number of his chips to get approval for the church-growth program and it hadn't worked. He had no idea what to do next and doubted that he would ever be able to move the church off dead center and see the kind of growth that the congregation, his denominational executives, and, more important, that he desired to see. He felt like a failure. *What had gone wrong,* he wondered? Where had he failed to implement the program properly? Surely they had overlooked some important detail. He just couldn't put his finger on the problem.

My young pastor friend's attempt to produce church growth by following a recipe that had promised significant results had precipitated a personal ministry crisis that would require more than a year for him to completely overcome. Surprisingly, in spite of this failed attempt at formulaic church growth, Curt was not done searching for the right recipe. During the years following this ministry debacle, after time had sufficiently eroded his feelings of failure, he tried his hand at yet another "growth" program—experiencing only slightly better results. After five years of ministry in that church, Curt left for another ministry opportunity. Obviously, Curt reasoned, he was not the pastor whom God intended to use to bring growth to that particular church. His church-growth success still had to be out there somewhere and he was determined to find it. Unfortunately, ten years after leaving that first church, Curt's big success is yet to materialize.

A Survey of Formulas for Ministry Success

Anyone who has been in ministry for any length of time can no doubt relate in many respects to Curt's experience. Like Curt, I too have tried numerous surefire methods down through the years that promised to produce significant church growth, only to be left frustrated and even, at times, angry with the congregation God had called me to serve.

Because in the last twenty-five years numerical growth has become one of the primary measures of pastoral success, countless seminars, tool kits, programs, philosophies, and methodologies have been spawned, promising to produce the much-coveted product of church growth.

The Phone's for You

While I was serving as a church-planting pastor during the late 1980s, there was a literal smorgasbord of church-growth formulas from which to choose. One of the programs that I embraced was called "The Phone's for You." This church-growth formula was based on what is called "the law of large numbers." According to this program the secret to church growth success was simply calling a large enough number of people and inviting them to church. The Phone's for You promised that if you followed the plan and made the requisite number of "dial-ups," you would see consistent results of 1 percent favorable response. For example, if you wanted to see 200 new people in church on a given Sunday, all you had to do was make 200,000 dial-ups. This number of dial-ups would ensure that you got your 1 percent positive response—200 new people in church.

31

I conducted this program at least twice during my tenure as a church planter. Though we never came near to the results that the program creators promised, we did receive some positive benefits. The effort created a sense of team among our members and a mutual commitment to a common cause that helped our infant congregation in ways that were less tangible than actual numerical growth. However, the people that responded to our phoning efforts generally tended to wander off after only several weeks of attendance. But, in fairness, we did add a few folks who became regular attendees. Still, most of those people were already believers who had left another church in frustration or who had recently moved to our area from elsewhere. The number of nonchurched people we reached through this program ended up being nominal at best.

Now with that said, I am not suggesting that The Phone's for You was an ineffective ministry tool. It was somewhat useful, but it was not a formula for instant church growth. Most of the pastors I know who have utilized this tool have done so with the expectation that it would deliver as promised. This was certainly my expectation. We were not using this tool primarily for team building among our core group or for getting people involved in ministry, though those were peripheral benefits. The chief reason we invested the thousands of dollars required to effectively conduct the calling campaign was because it promised to deliver instant growth. That's just the honest, carnal truth! But like my friend Curt, we were all underwhelmed by our results and were quick to move on to the next program that promised growth. And there were plenty of programs from which to choose.

Most of the pastors I know have tried one or more of these programs at one time or another. Let's consider just a partial sampling of some of these church-growth methodologies and programs that will probably be familiar to most church leaders.

Expository Preaching

During the early 1980s, as the churches of great expositors, such as Chuck Swindoll, John MacArthur, David Hocking, and Gordon MacDonald, began to experience phenomenal growth, expository preaching was promoted as the key to rapid church growth. If the pastor would focus on producing and delivering sound expository messages, his church could expect numerical growth.

I do not want to imply that expository preaching is not an essential element to holistic church growth—I believe it is—it's just that it is not some fail-safe formula for church growth. I don't believe the pastors previously mentioned ever intended to promote expository preaching as a formula. But pastors hungry for success and numerical growth were quick to latch on to it because they saw the fruit enjoyed by some pastors who used it. While expository preaching is vital to spiritual development and health, it is not a recipe for certain growth.

Church Marketing

Another popular methodology that was in vogue during the end of the 1980s and on into the early '90s was church marketing. This formula for church growth promoted the concept of doing market research in an effort to understand the demographic makeup of a church's ministry area and then developing a ministry that would meet the needs of the population on which the church would focus its ministry efforts.

Once a target group was selected and their felt needs identified, the church could then implement an effective strategy for marketing their ministry and programs to the target population. This would be done through creative advertising; high-impact, need-oriented messages; and special-attraction programs that were certain to woo the target audience into the church.

Again I am not suggesting that there is no merit to some of the methodologies promoted by the church-marketing approach. I am simply saying that it is not the formula for guaranteed church growth that many pastors hoped it would be and that some promoted it to be.

Seeker-Sensitive Services

Observing the staggering growth experienced by Willow Creek Community Church and Saddleback Community Church, many pastors and church leaders were drawn to the seeker-sensitive approach that has been so successfully employed by uniquely gifted pastors like Bill Hybels and Rick Warren.

During the late 1980s and throughout the 1990s, the seeker-sensitive model eclipsed in popularity and execution all other models and methodologies for church growth. In an effort to see results similar to those at Willow Creek and Saddleback, countless pastors were quick to try the seeker-sensitive techniques and ministry approach of these churches, attempting to duplicate them in their own setting. Unfortunately, many of these pastors were ministering in the context of one-hundred-year-old churches with a long tradition of worship and ministry programs quite foreign to the seeker-sensitive model. As many of these pastors attempted to introduce wholesale change from the traditional model to the seeker-sensitive approach, their efforts frequently resulted in no little tumult within the ranks of many churches and denominations. In fact this movement toward implementing a more seeker-sensitive approach in churches steeped in historic traditions has resulted in the heightening of the worship wars that have been ravaging so many churches during recent years.

Though extremely effective at reaching people for Christ in many contexts, the seeker-sensitive (or seeker-driven) model is not a guaranteed formula for ministry success for every church, and I don't believe Bill Hybels or Rick Warren ever intended to communicate that message.

At the August 2000 Willow Creek Leadership Summit, Bill Hybels suggested that the current seeker-sensitive format has begun to lose its effectiveness and is in need of rethinking for the twenty-first century. It's not that there is anything wrong with the seeker-sensitive model of ministry. It's just that in the current form popularized by Willow Creek, it has run its course.

The leaders of Willow Creek recognize that the seeker-sensitive format is not appropriate in every church setting. And they've seen that too many pastors today are looking for a silver bullet that will produce instant ministry success.

Rather than engaging in the excruciating spadework of prayer, study, dialogue, and testing over a period of time to discern what God might want to do in their ministry environment, these pastors want a ready-made methodology that is guaranteed to work.

Aware of this simplistic tendency, Willow Creek repeatedly cautions pastors and leaders not to rush home from one of their seminars and attempt to force a one-size-fits-all methodology on their church. But still, in spite of the warnings, many pastors are so eager to see some tangible signs of growth that they unwisely forge ahead anyway.

35

Seven-Day-a-Week Churches

A more recent formula for church growth has been the promotion of what are being called seven-day-a-week churches. This model of ministry promotes the creation of a plethora of relevant ministries that keep the church active and functioning throughout the week. This concept for church growth is based on the idea that in a culture where the church is forced to compete with the mall, sporting events, movie theaters, and so many other attractions, the church must create a similar menu of program choices and activities to draw people.

In addition to these more popular formulas for church growth, there is an almost endless list of variations that have been promoted both intentionally and unintentionally: bus ministries, small groups, transitioning, purpose-driven mission development, support groups, visioning, Fuller Seminary's Breaking the Barriers series of seminars, and numerous other programs and methodologies. Many have believed that these hold the secrets to church growth. Unless there are some significant changes in the culture of the evangelical church in America during the twenty-first century, it is safe to assume that new methods and formulas will continue to emerge.

First-Century Church-Growth Formulas

It's interesting to note that, in spite of the current emphasis on the various formulas for ministry success, the Scriptures are all but silent on the subject of church growth. As you survey the New Testament writings of the apostle Paul, you can't help but be struck by the stark absence of any advice or specific recommendations that even remotely resemble today's church-growth strategies. Instead, there seems to be an almost obsessive focus on faithfulness in ministry and standing firm against the pervasive pull of a crumbling and godless culture. There is nothing said about attempting to appeal to popular culture. On the contrary, there seems to be a strong emphasis on remaining free from the influence of culture and focusing on the simple proclamation of the "foolish" gospel.

In the Pastoral Epistles, where one would expect to find advice for helping the church grow, Paul's emphasis is almost exclusively on encouraging church leaders to lead a godly life and assist their congregations in doing the same. If they would do this, live a life that was worthy of their calling in Christ, Paul knew that their example would provide powerful confirmation of the gospel realities that they preached.

In 1 Corinthians 2:1–5 the apostle Paul says to the church leaders:

> Dear brothers and sisters, when I first came to you I didn't use lofty words and brilliant ideas to tell you God's message. For I decided to concentrate only on Jesus Christ and his death on the cross. I came to you in weakness—timid and trembling. And my message and my preaching were very plain. I did not use wise and persuasive speeches, but the Holy Spirit was powerful among you. I did this so that you might trust the power of God rather than human wisdom.

Rather than giving advice on how to grow the church, Paul seems to discount the impact of human ingenuity and technique, attributing the growth of the church in Corinth to the presence of the Spirit powerfully at work among them. Paul specifically says he chose not to employ brilliant ideas in bringing them the gospel, but

37

rather he had determined to deliver the message in straightforward simplicity, relying on the power of God to make the message effective and produce growth.

Later in this same letter Paul actually admonishes and scolds the Christians at Corinth because of their apparent tendency to latch on to the techniques and methodologies of different leaders and teachers:

> When one of you says, "I am a follower of Paul," and another says, "I prefer Apollos," aren't you acting like those who are not Christians? Who is Apollos, and who is Paul, that we should be the cause of such quarrels? Why, we're only servants. Through us God caused you to believe. Each of us did the work the Lord gave us. My job was to plant the seed in your hearts, and Apollos watered it, *but it was God, not we, who made it grow.* The ones who do the planting or watering aren't important, *but God is important because he is the one who makes the seed grow.*
>
> 1 Corinthians 3:4–7

Paul's words almost sound as if they could be addressed to a present-day gathering of pastors or denominational leaders. Today there seems to be all sorts of quarreling among pastors and Christian leaders stemming from preferred strategies for church growth and advancement. Today the quarrels would be more along the lines of "I am of seeker-sensitive"; "I am of purpose-driven"; "I am of Church Next." Or maybe "I am of Hybels"; "I am of Piper"; "I am of Warren." In response to our tendency to eagerly cling to the latest church-growth formula or ministry approach, Paul's message would be the same to us as it was to the leaders at Corinth when he said, "The ones who do the planting and the watering aren't important, but God is important because he is the one who makes the seed grow."

The truth is, if we're willing to be gut-level honest with ourselves and God, there have been many times when we have placed more faith in the current technique or formula we were using in an effort to produce growth than we have in God. How easy it is in this day and age to get caught up in placing more attention on our formulas for success and growth than we do on the supernatural working of the Holy Spirit among and through us! The questions we must answer are: Where is our focus? On what are we relying for ultimate success and the growth of the church?

Though it is true that Paul was singularly reliant on the power of Christ for his ministry effectiveness, he also employed different methods of proclamation at different times and with different audiences, such as his encounter at the Areopagus in Athens recorded in Acts 17.

We're also familiar with Paul's words in 1 Corinthians when he writes:

> When I am with the Jews, I become one of them so that I can bring them to Christ. When I am with those who follow the Jewish laws, I do the same, even though I am not subject to the law, so that I can bring them to Christ. When I am with the Gentiles who do not have the Jewish law, I fit in with them as much as I can. In this way, I gain their confidence and bring them to Christ. But I do not discard the law of God; I obey the law of Christ. . . . Yes, I try to find common ground with everyone so that I might bring them to Christ. I do all this to spread the Good News, and in doing so I enjoy its blessings.
>
> 1 Corinthians 9:20–23

It seems clear that Paul was quick to use different methods in preaching the gospel. I am not saying in all of this that we should not attempt creative and new ways of reaching people with the Good News of freedom from sin

39

and new life in Christ. What I am saying, however, is that whenever we reduce these various methodologies into formulas for success, place more confidence in them than we do in the simple power of the gospel; or when we find ourselves thinking that some program or formula will *cause* our church to grow and be the source of success, we are setting ourselves up for failure and frustration.

In their book *How to Change Your Church without Killing It,* authors Gene Appel and Alan Nelson state:

> Throughout history, people have taken a new thing God was doing and elevated it to an unhealthy level, so much so that their affections became attached to the method instead of to God. . . . We do not believe that every church is called to be a large congregation. We have been associated with large churches that were not healthy in terms of reaching the lost in their community and communicating with relevance. . . . Too much emphasis is often placed on the super-growth models of local congregations that cause undue pressure on others to "perform." Churches of one thousand or more in attendance make up a minuscule fraction of congregations.[1]

We need to always remember that it is God and God alone who is the source of genuine church growth. God and God alone is the causal agent in the type of church growth that took place in the Book of Acts and the early church.

It was God who brought about the phenomenal growth of Willow Creek, not the seeker-sensitive strategies used by the church. For whatever reason, in the case of Willow Creek, God chose to work through this unique methodology and the leaders who implemented it after a serious time of prayer and reflection. It does not follow, then, that every other church that uses the methods of Willow Creek will experience the same kind of result that they have.

Willow Creek is unique in the kingdom of God. The leadership of Bill Hybels, the context of the church's founding, as well as its geographic and cultural setting, are all unique to this church. Why would we expect God to produce the same results in our ministry context? It makes no sense.

Our job is not to discover the right formula and then attempt to flawlessly implement it. Rather, our job as leaders of God's church is to listen for God's voice and determine what he is calling us to do in our unique ministry setting. Church growth is not simply a matter of purchasing the latest ministry tool kit and then putting it to use. Church growth is a much more dynamic and spiritual process than that.

The danger for us as pastors and spiritual leaders today lies not so much in the methodologies that we employ as it does in the attitude and focus of our heart as we employ them. When, like Paul, we employ culturally sensitive methods and techniques, knowing that God will use them to serve his sovereign purposes and not merely to satisfy our need for success, then we will find a measure of serenity and fulfillment regardless of the outcome or numerical result.

But, when we place too much faith in the formulas and methodologies themselves, believing they will produce the success and growth for which we yearn, we will discover that they are formulas for nothing but frustration.

The Wild Card of God's Sovereignty

We need to understand that the wild card in all of our efforts at church growth is the sovereignty of God. God

41

causes the church to grow for his own pleasure and to advance his sovereign purposes not ours.

God does not feel constrained to act in ways that are always consistent with the latest church-growth formulas and methods. Just because he blessed one church that did a certain thing does not in any way mean that he will produce the same result for every other church that employs the same methods. The sooner we come to grips with the role of God's sovereignty over the growth and expansion of his church, the sooner we will begin to more consistently experience a measure of serenity and joy in the exercise of our ministry, regardless of the tangible outcomes.

I am convinced that even as difficult and challenging as ministry is in the twenty-first century, those of us who have been called by God to labor in his field should experience a deep sense of fulfillment and serenity in spite of the battles we must fight and the apparent lack of tangible growth we must periodically endure.

If we are ever going to experience that kind of ministry, however, it will require that we acknowledge, understand, and then address the constant battle we must wage between our own need for personal success and the sovereign plans of God. For many spiritual leaders there is a continuing tension between realizing personal success and embracing the sovereignty of God. It is to the understanding of that battle we now turn in chapter 3.

Suggestions for Self-Reflection

1. Take a few minutes to list some of the different formulaic approaches to church growth that you have tried at one time or another. What were the results for each of the formulas you executed?

2. When was the last time you took a multiple-day personal retreat to reflect on God's purpose for your church and the strategies he might want you to employ in realizing his purpose? What makes taking a personal retreat in search of God's purpose and direction difficult, while following a formula developed by another pastor in another place seems easy?

3. Why do you think that the apostle Paul didn't share more specific strategies for church growth when writing to young pastors in his New Testament letters? What conclusions can you draw from this?

4. Why do we often react adversely to the statement, "God doesn't care about our success, only our faithfulness"?

5. Reread 1 Corinthians 3:4–7. In your own words, what was God saying through the apostle Paul about the nature of church growth? Do you believe that twenty-first-century church leaders truly embrace the truth of Paul's statement in verse 7? Why or why not?

6. What is the critical difference between what Paul writes in 1 Corinthians 3:4–7 and what he writes a few chapters later in 9:20–23? Read them both again and give your own assessment.

7. Respond to the statement, "The wild card in all of church growth is the sovereignty of God." What does that mean to you and how do you react to it?

THREE

Personal Ministry Success
versus
God's Sovereignty

An Uneasy Paradox

The call came near midnight. I was retreating in the mountains of southern California with another ministry colleague, planning for the upcoming year of ministry, when the phone rang in the borrowed cabin where we were staying.

On the other end of the line was a member of a call committee for a medium-sized church in the Midwest. His church was in search of a leader who could bring change to their stagnant, 120-year-old congregation. He had received my name from a mutual contact and wanted to know if I would be interested in candidating as their senior pastor.

Having never lived east of Idaho and being quite happy in the church I'd planted in southern California, I was not interested by the offer. I declined but prayed with the man, asking God to direct the search committee to just the right person for the position. As we concluded our conversation, the committee member asked if I would be willing to send a videotape of one of our services. The committee was simply interested in seeing what was happening out there in the "contemporary" church world.

Two weeks later I received another call. This time it was the chairman of the call committee. He apologized awkwardly for the call but said their committee felt led to contact me again, feeling I was just the type of person for whom they were looking. He wanted to know if I would at least be willing to talk with their committee over the phone. Well, to make a long story short, I ended up accepting that position after nearly six months of visits, interviews, question-and-answer sessions, and a congregational meeting at which I received a 97 percent vote.

I accepted the position for a variety of reasons. Chief among them was the fact that I felt confident God was calling us to serve this conservative, Midwestern congregation. Another convincing reason included the feeling that it was an opportunity at which I could succeed. I felt sure that the skills, experiences, and tools I had obtained in the church-planting trenches would enable me to bring the positive change to the church that the call committee and elder board were anxious to see—more conversions, numerical growth, a more contemporary worship style.

After my first six months at the church I began to realize the magnitude of the challenge facing me. I could see that turning this church around was going to be a monumental task. But still, I felt sure that with hard work, savvy leadership, and congregational support the job the Lord had called me to do would get done. After months of studying the church's history, giving trends,

45

attendance records, as well as the demographics of the area, it became clear that if we were going to see the kind of congregational change we desired, it would require us to relocate the church.

In my mind's eye I could see the future for this church. I could actually envision new people sitting in the congregation. I could hear the music we'd be playing and could clearly see a new facility located in a rapidly expanding area of our city. I could imagine our revitalized church reaching out in aggressive evangelism to our new community and confidently anticipated that people would respond positively to our efforts. It was going to be an exciting, challenging, and, I was sure, exhausting experience. Little did I know that my years at this church would prove to be among the most difficult, personally painful, and spiritually trying seasons of my life.

I had accepted this position to succeed. I didn't move my family across the country and leave the denomination in which I had been ordained just to survive and maintain the status quo at this new ministry. And I had every reason to believe that the church would succeed at our relocation and revitalization endeavor.

Up to this point in my life everything I had attempted in ministry had been successful. Our church-planting effort in California had grown from a mere handful of committed and faithful people to nearly 800 people who attended my last Easter service there. We had added staff and acquired our own facility. We provided some of the best worship music in our region of southern California, and our worship leader was writing original music that was both stunning and inspiring. In fact today she is a nationally known Christian recording artist.

In addition to my successful attempt at church planting, my first ministry position out of seminary had been unquestionably successful. As an associate pastor at that church, I was able to develop a very successful education program built around the church's mission statement. After all, it was my successful ministry track record that had ultimately led the call committee to pursue me in the first place. That's why they wanted me; they wanted to see success as much as I did.

But in spite of my record of success, personal determination, spiritual giftedness, and ministry experience I ended up leaving that church after just six years feeling like an unmitigated failure. In fact my failure at this church left me wounded and shaken to my very soul. During my final years of ministry there, I became so depressed my wife finally convinced me to see a psychiatrist to get help. The diagnosis: serious depression.

Up to that point in my life and ministry I rarely experienced a down day—the glass was always half full from my perspective. But something happened inside of me as I vainly struggled to see success at that church, something I couldn't understand let alone explain. By the time we actually left that ministry, I had begun to question my calling, my giftedness, and even the level of my commitment to Christ as a result of this ministry debacle—at least what I considered a debacle.

Let me explain. We did relocate the church to the fastest growing part of our city. We were able to pay cash for seventeen acres of prime property right in the heart of all the development. We were able to add skilled and highly qualified staff. We had over two hundred thousand dollars in the bank toward our new facility. We even succeeded in changing the name of the church to something more "user friendly." In addition to all of that, during those six years we experienced the highest attendance and giving in the 120-year history of that church.

So why, you might ask, was this such a life-shattering experience for me? How could these achievements have resulted in a period of serious depression and disillusionment? What went so terribly wrong that I would be caused to question my calling to ministry?

Sadly, the reason for my feelings of failure was that I had not achieved the level of success I had envisioned for myself and that church, and the little success that we did see was not happening fast enough for me. Remember, I had envisioned what success would look like for that church. I had established predetermined benchmarks for my success in that ministry setting. I knew what had to happen for me to "feel" like I had succeeded at the task for which I had been hired.

Because my expectations didn't materialize in the way or to the extent I had hoped, I felt like a failure. We hadn't become the large, outreach-oriented church I envisioned. Though we were seeing growth, it wasn't the record-setting growth I had anticipated. And because there was grumbling and constant complaining among some of the church's older, powerful members, I felt we would never become the church I had envisioned. So I left with my tail tucked between my legs, my confidence shaken, feeling that my successful ministry track record had been tarnished.

Caught in a Culture of Success

Today we live in a culture of success. More to the point, Americans seem to worship at the altar of success. Everywhere you turn, there is an emphasis on success—in our work, as a person (whatever that means!), financial, or in creating and building an organization.

Success and all of its secrets are constantly paraded before us, tempting us at every turn to sell our soul for our piece of the American dream. And, unfortunately, as Christians we are not in any way immune from the intoxicating effects of today's success syndrome. The same culture of success that has permeated American society since the '70s and '80s has become equally as influential in evangelical circles and among the leaders who serve the American church. Though it is true that the desire to be successful has always been a part of the human experience, it was during the 1970s and '80s that success took on a decidedly acquisitive shape. During the last thirty years it seems success has become something that must be quantified to be real. Money, homes, titles, earnings per share, and even congregational growth seem to have become the currency of true success. It's no longer just possessing or experiencing these things that makes a successful person, but rather how much of them we possess or experience.

It used to be that just owning a home—any home—made you a success. At one time having a healthy marriage, possessing a good work ethic, being honest and moral, as well as exhibiting other intangible character qualities were indisputable indicators of success. But today a person can be hollow on the inside and void of previously indispensable character traits and still be considered a role model for success as long as he or she has lots of money, power, fame, a large home, or a coveted position (take for example many of our culture's politicians, athletes, and entertainers).

And so, with the emergence of the megachurch, it seems that we as Christian leaders have also begun measuring our success with a predominantly quantitative standard of measure. It's no longer simply serving as a pastor that makes a person successful. Now we must pastor a large, rapidly growing church—at least that seems to be the direction we have been moving in recent years.

All through seminary and during my years as a pastor—almost twenty as of this writing—I have been exposed to an ever-increasing number of ministry leaders who have attained celebrity status and a certain spiritual "star" quality in evangelical circles, primarily because their churches have grown numerically. Being constantly exposed to these ministry stars in Christian magazines, ministry seminars, radio programs, books, arena events, and television programs, somewhere along the way I, like many, subtly began to equate true success with the attainment of similar status.

Though the development and expansion of the various forms of media have increased our ability to spread the gospel, the downside is that media tend to glamorize the ministry and transform those who utilize such high-profile tools into Christian celebrities of sorts. Unfortunately, for many leaders looking for affirmation and personal worth, this media-created celebrity can become something that is subtly sought as an end in itself rather than as a by-product of communicating the gospel.

I wasn't blatantly grasping for similar spiritual stardom, but a longing for more substantial success began to lurk beneath the surface of my life, often surreptitiously motivating my ministry efforts. It seemed perfectly legitimate to me. After all, the pathway to such status and its attendant success could only be achieved by building an effective, growing, marquee-type ministry that could then be held up as a template that other churches could use as a model.

Though it is not something I am proud of and am pained even now to write this, much of my ministry effort over the years has been subtly driven by the quest for success—my own personal success. But because I have always been able to cloak these intentions in kingdom language, and because most of the leaders I have served with have also defined success in similar terms and have been as desperate as I to see it, I was never really forced to come to grips with my inner strivings for success and personal advancement. It wasn't until my failure at revitalizing this church, and being forced to sift through the spiritual rubble left in its wake, that I had to take a long, hard look at what had been motivating my ministry for too many years.

It was because of my perceived failure that I have taken the last couple of years to reflect on why I have never experienced the level of joy and serenity in ministry the apostle Paul wrote about while sitting in a Roman prison cell, waiting for his head to be removed (see Phil. 4:11–13).

In stark contrast to the apostle Paul's experience, most of my years in ministry have been lived in nice, comfortable homes, serving churches with adequate facilities and significant resources, yet I have spent the majority of those years feeling frustrated and like a personal failure.

The last word I would have ever thought of using to describe my years in ministry would be *serene*. At no time in the past would I have been able to say I felt truly content and completely satisfied with the fruits of my labor. Oh, there may have been some fleeting moments of tranquillity through those years, but certainly not enough to honestly say that my ministry has been characterized by a sense of deep inner satisfaction and serenity.

It was at Eagle Heights Church, in Omaha, Nebraska, that my strivings for personal success collided headlong with the realities of God's sovereignty, and it was an extremely painful and sobering collision—a collision that could have been avoided. It could have been avoided, though I would have undoubtedly at some time had a collision in some other area. Not all pastors struggle in exactly the same way. God provides different growth experiences for different people.

Success and the Sovereignty of God

There comes a time when those of us involved in ministry must come to grips with the awesome realities of God's sovereignty and the implications that it has for our own personal success.

For too many of us who are spiritual leaders, ministry can quickly be reduced to just another career or profession at which we can be successful and make a name for ourselves. For those with entrepreneurial leanings the temptation is strong to treat church planting as something akin to a business start-up—acquire the financing, develop a business plan, create a compelling marketing campaign, and voilà—a successful start-up!

When we begin to think this way, though, we become much too cavalier toward God's sovereignty and what we consider success in ministry. I'm afraid this entrepreneurial view of ministry can also make us much too demanding when it comes to the outcomes we expect our efforts to produce. Moreover, it is our failure to acknowledge the role of God's sovereignty in our ministry efforts that often results in so much frustration, feelings of failure, stress, and even, at times, intense anger as we slug it out in the ministry trenches.

We must realize that there are much greater forces at work in our ministry than simply our own will power, enthusiasm, determination, giftedness, vision, and passion. The reality is that the church in which we serve is God's church. And God has some very definite ideas of what success looks like in his church. In fact God has some very specific ideas of what success looks like for each one of us individually. It is not up to us to determine what will ultimately take place in the church we serve—that is God's job—and we forget or neglect that reality at our own emotional and spiritual peril. The same is true for our own life. Contrary to the current

52

prevailing opinion, we are not the masters of our own destiny. That is God's job. But because of the constant messages we receive from our culture, it is easy to forget that biblical truth and try to take control of our life.

Because God is sovereign in and over his church, he does not feel compelled to produce growth simply because we have determined that our church should grow and become a more expansive ministry. God is not constrained to produce health and spiritual vibrancy according to our personal timetable or just because we happen to be perfectly employing the latest church-growth theories. God does not grow the church to meet our desperate need for tangible results so that we can feel good about ourselves or have the assurance that we are succeeding in ministry.

Now, obviously, God does not desire churches to remain stagnant and plateaued. God is not in favor of ingrown, selfish churches that could care less about those who don't yet know Jesus Christ. God does desire to see his church growing and healthy, consistently reaching people with the good news of the gospel. After all, that is why he sent his Son to earth, to seek and to save those who are lost.

As shocking as it may be to some of us—in fact it may sound to some like outright heresy—I do not believe God is all that concerned with our own needs for personal success—at least not as we often define success. God is much more concerned that his name be glorified and honored in the church and in all the earth than he is with whether or not we "feel" successful. God grows the church to fulfill his own purposes and for his own good pleasure. And very often in ministry there come times when we experience a direct and powerful clash between our needs for personal success and the sovereign actions of God.

It is at the point of that clash when we often find ourselves struggling in ministry and frustrated that things are not happening the way we had planned or as quickly as we would like. And it is precisely at this point that we must acknowledge and embrace the reality of God's sovereignty and find a measure of serenity in the knowledge that God is in control not only of our church but also of our life and ministry.

No matter how chaotic or out of control our life may seem at any given time, God is strategically at work. He has a plan and purpose for each of us. Unfortunately, our personal plan is often at odds with God's sovereign purposes for our life and work. When the plans we have laid out for our life and our pursuit of personal success conflict with God's sovereign plans and purpose for us, we will need to acquiesce and search out what God's direction for us might be. We can do this by listening to God, reflecting, seeking spiritual direction, letting go of a personal dream that might be blocking us from seeing God's direction for us, or by allowing our dream to take a different shape based on the circumstances God allows into our life. We cannot expect God's sovereign plan to change.

Often because we have a predetermined plan for our life or our church and think we know what success looks like, we lobby God to get him to participate with us in what we want to do and think is best. When God refuses to satisfy our demands, we can become frustrated, begin to pout, blame the congregation or others, and engage in a whole host of selfish and spiritually immature behaviors.

Though the Scriptures seem crystal clear about the reality that God's plans cannot be thwarted and that his purposes do not always coincide with ours, it seems to be a wall that many of us in ministry continue to pound our heads against to no positive effect. Finding serenity in life and ministry will require that we embrace the sovereignty of God and willingly compromise our personal plans when they seem to be in conflict with what God is doing. God has promised that the gates of hell cannot stand against the expansion of his church. Therefore if our church is not experiencing the success we desire, it must be because of our own sinfulness (James 1) or the sovereignty of God.

Relinquishing Our Personal Plans

As a young man Saul of Tarsus had planned a career path for himself that would land him a position of power and prestige. Saul had set his sights on achieving significant personal success. He climbed the ecclesiastical ladder and was well on his way to realizing his personal goals when his life was turned upside down on the Damascus Road. Though he had already achieved a level of enviable success in his chosen profession (see Phil. 3:4–7), God had other plans for Saul of Tarsus.

We know well the story of Saul's traumatic encounter with the risen Jesus on the Damascus Road. At the very heart of this historic encounter was a confrontation between Saul's personal plans for his life and God's sovereign plan for him. The crux of the confrontation takes place in Acts 9:5 when Jesus says to Saul, "I am Jesus, the one you are persecuting! Now get up and go into the city, and you will be told what you are to do." At that moment God was interrupting Saul's well-laid plans for his life. Even at the point of this encounter, Saul is on a mission that will increase his reputation among the Pharisees. But suddenly he is faced with a major decision: Will he let go of his personal life plan and his vision of what success looked like, to respond to this divine interruption? Or will Saul insist on following the course he had set for himself, rejecting God's purposes for him? At that moment in Saul's life, there was a very real decision to be made, a decision that would in large measure determine the future quality of his life as well as his feelings of significance and success.

As we know, Saul chose to relent when his plans smacked into the sovereignty of God. I'm absolutely certain that at that point Saul was confused and concerned about what was transpiring in his life. But in spite of Saul's uncertainty about what his future might look like, God was in sovereign control of his life and was in the process of bringing about a future ministry that would stagger even Saul.

In Acts 9:15 the Lord reveals his plan for Saul's life when he says to Ananias: "Go and do what I say. For Saul is my chosen instrument to take my message to the Gentiles and to kings, as well as to the people of Israel. And I will show him how much he must suffer for me."

Later in his life, after Saul of Tarsus had become Paul the apostle and he was able to see his life from God's sovereign perspective, he tells the Galatians: "For it pleased God in his kindness to choose me and call me, even before I was born! What undeserved mercy! Then he revealed his Son to me so that I could proclaim the Good News about Jesus to the Gentiles" (Gal. 1:15–16).

Now without question Paul's life as an apostle was much less comfortable and successful from a human perspective than it would have been had he remained a prominent Pharisee. As a result of acquiescing to God's intervention in his life, Paul changed from the one doing the persecuting to the one being persecuted. By allowing God to interrupt his personal plans, he became an itinerant evangelist and church planter who was forced to rely on tent-making to meet many of his physical and material needs—not exactly what we would call an upwardly mobile career choice!

But Paul had also experienced the pain and frustration that comes from fighting against God's sovereign will. In Acts 26:14, as Paul recounts for King Agrippa his experience on the Damascus Road and how he had been resisting God's sovereign actions in his life, he recalls how the risen Jesus had said to him, "Saul, Saul, why are you persecuting me? It is hard for you to fight against my will."

It seems that during the course of his life and ministry Paul had come to grips with the tension that always seems to exist between our own personal plans and God's sovereign plans for us.

In Romans 9 Paul explains that we are in no position to question God's sovereign purposes for us or how he chooses to use us to further his kingdom and advance his own name: "For the Scriptures say that God told Pharaoh, 'I have appointed you for the very purpose of displaying my power in you, and so that my fame might spread throughout the earth' " (Rom. 9:17).

Like the Romans of Paul's day, most of us who have been brought up in a culture that emphasizes personal choice and the freedom of self-determination bristle at the unfairness and apparent randomness of such a statement. We don't much care for the idea that we are not in complete control of our own destiny. It actually disturbs us to think that there might be outside forces at work determining the extent of our success and the shape our achievement takes. In fact current American culture considers such notions as absolute anathema, the worst possible sort of life philosophy. But Paul responds to such reactions when he states:

> Who are you, a mere human being, to criticize God? Should the thing that was created say to the one who made it, "Why have you made me like this?" When a potter makes jars out of clay, doesn't he have a right to use

57

the same lump of clay to make one jar for decoration and another to throw garbage into? God has every right to exercise his judgment and his power.

Romans 9:20–22

I wonder if we have reached the point in our life and ministry where we can say that we are content and at peace with however God may choose to use us in his kingdom work. Are we able to release our visions of megachurch magnificence in favor of allowing God to have his way with us, regardless of what that may mean for our own personal plans? Can we let go of our plans of becoming a nationally known speaker or writer in favor of God-ordained anonymity and an unrelenting faithfulness to follow the calling he has planted deep within our heart regardless of the outcome for us personally? God does not measure success in the same way we do. It is often through what appears to be the greatest human failures and tragedies that God is most directly at work bringing about his sovereign purposes for his church and for us.

Even Jesus himself, God in human flesh, came to the place where he had to say, "I want your will, not mine." This is a concession that we are often quick to give lip service to in our journal and prayers, but inwardly there is an ongoing struggle to make it a reality in the way we live.

Jesus could have done things his way, or he could choose to relinquish his will to the Father. By letting go of his own human will, Jesus allowed the Father's will to be done and it resulted in the best possible outcome for the largest possible number of people.

Are we able to believe that God knows what he is doing and trust him even in the darkness of what may feel like personal failure despite our best efforts? As we will see in chapter five, trusting God is the key to finding the serenity and significance that we so desperately desire.

What will it take for you to reach the place in your life and ministry where you are truly more concerned with God's purposes and plans for you and your church than you are with your own plans? For me it has been a lifelong and, at times, very painful battle—a battle I have not yet entirely won. It is for me an ongoing struggle, though I can honestly say that I have now reached a place in my life where I can usually say I want God to use me in whatever way he desires. But it has taken me quite some time to say even that much. Like Paul, however, I also have had to learn the hard way how difficult and personally painful it can be to fight against the sovereign will of God in favor of my own will.

One lesson that moved me in this direction was my experience at Eagle Heights that I described at the beginning of this chapter. But still it is an ongoing challenge for me to "seek first his kingdom" rather than pursue my own personal agenda for success.

Another lesson in submitting to God's will came a couple of years ago when I was going through a restless period in my life and ministry. God has given me a passion to write and communicate publicly. He has also placed within me a desire to work in the area of leadership formation in an effort to develop whole and healthy leaders who will finish well. As I have already confessed, I also have a healthy desire for success and achievement.

During this period of restlessness I began to contemplate leaving the pastoral ministry for a ministry of writing and speaking on the issues about which I am passionate. In retrospect, one of the factors that was making such a ministry change seem extremely palatable was the fact that I was taking some "hits" in my

59

church as a result of some minor changes that were being made.

My natural inclination during that period was to pursue a change in ministry venue. I felt I could be more successful, have increased freedom, endure less criticism, and earn significantly more money—all very enticing benefits—just by changing my ministry. I would be working in an area of my God-given passion in a ministry I had previously been encouraged to pursue by other colleagues and supporters. For some time I had sensed that God would at some point lead me into a speaking and writing ministry. But as I contemplated it as an immediate pursuit, I had a low-grade, inner gnawing that all was not well with such a decision.

In an effort to gain some spiritual clarity I spent a few days in North Carolina with my spiritual director and friend Leighton Ford. During our time together he created an environment in which God was able to help me see that the time for such a move was not right, that maybe God was at work doing something else in my life. Leighton encouraged me to listen more closely for the voice and direction of God deep within my spirit before I made any decision.

Ultimately I came to the realization that I was not to leave my church. I realized that though my desires and passions for writing and leadership formation were legitimate—indeed God-born—my forging ahead would be untimely and selfish. It would be a decision made more for my own personal advancement and the building of my personal kingdom than for the advancement of God's kingdom through the ministry of the local church to which I had been called.

Had I forged ahead stubbornly, which I have been known to do on occasion, I would have created a significant mess in my life, the life of my family, and the life of my church. I realize that some day God may lead me into a speaking and writing ministry, but at that time it was not the appropriate decision for me. I have had to learn to hold that dream loosely and wait on God's timing.

I wish I could say I have always exercised such sound judgment when faced with a conflict between my personal plans and the sovereignty of God. Unfortunately, if I were entirely honest, I would have to admit that I am much more familiar with the pain that comes from resisting God's will in favor of my own. And it has been at those times of willful resistance that I have experienced a collision much like the apostle Paul's on the Damascus Road, as God got my attention in the only way that would work at the time. But I am learning that it doesn't always have to be that way.

I have slowly begun to learn that when I am willing to completely release my life to God and hold my personal aspirations loosely, God never fails to bring into my life the very opportunities and outcomes that I had been working so hard for in my own strength. And though the things that God brings into my life do not always look exactly like what I had envisioned, they are always exceedingly better!

Understanding Our Drive to Succeed

It is important to recognize the tension that exists between our aspiring to personal success and significance on the one hand and desiring to do God's will on the other hand. This is one of those paradoxes that we may never fully understand this side of eternity. But it is a paradox with which we must continue to grapple throughout our life and ministry nonetheless.

As I have struggled with the tension between my will and God's will over the last ten years, I have become con-

vinced that our passionate desire for success and significance are among God's greatest gifts to us. He is the
one who has planted deep within us the desire to succeed and make a difference with our life. He has given
us our passions and the aspirations to better our life and
the lives of others.[1]

If God is the source of our passions and aspirations,
we can be sure that he has given them to us for a reason. He desires that we use them to seek out his purpose, not our own purposes, for our life. God has given
us an innate desire to achieve so that we can move
throughout our life toward the good things that he has
planned for us to do before we were even born.

Paul realized later in his life that, even before he was
born, God had a specific work for him to do (see Gal.
1:15). I believe Paul teaches that the same is true for
each of us who have been adopted into God's family. In
Ephesians 2:10 Paul says, "For we are God's masterpiece. He has created us anew in Christ Jesus, so that
we can do the good things he planned for us long ago."
And I have become increasingly convinced that it is this
passion and drive within us that God uses to keep us
moving toward discovering his sovereign purposes and
plans for us.

As I have already mentioned, I am an avid upland bird
hunter. I thoroughly enjoy exploring the vast reaches of
the Great Plains in search of game birds. Now finding
these little creatures in such expansive country is difficult at best. That is why virtually all serious bird hunters
have bird dogs.

My bird dog is a Brittany named Ginger. Now Ginger
has been bred for one purpose—to find birds. She has
an ability to scent birds that has been bred into her over
the course of many generations. Her sense of smell is a
homing device that is impossible to arrest once you have
released her in a field that contains birds. She has been

created to find them! But Ginger has two choices once I release her to find birds: She can hunt for me, staying in range and working ground that I can't cover, or she can hunt for herself. When she begins to hunt for herself, she simply takes off at top speed, allowing the intoxicating scent of wild birds to overwhelm her and pull her in every direction. She succumbs to this urge because it brings her pleasure—she enjoys searching for birds. But when she hunts for herself, it is very unproductive and makes my hunting extremely frustrating.

To help her overcome the urge to follow her instincts and hunt for herself, I purchased an electric training device (a shock collar to the hunting neophyte) and placed it around her neck before we began to hunt. At the first sign she was beginning to hunt for herself and running off course, I would give her a little electrical zap and the pain would get her attention and remind her that she was supposed to be finding birds for me, not just satisfying her instinctive urge. It didn't take too long before Ginger began to realize that the pain created by hunting for herself was no longer worth the excitement of following that natural urge. Instead she has learned to use her genetic scenting ability to find birds for me, her master. The result is that she enjoys her time in the field much more and so do I.

I believe the passions and aspirations God has given us are an awful lot like Ginger's inbred ability to scent birds. God has given them to us so that we can pursue significance and success in our endeavors. But God has not created us with an innate homing device for success and significance so that we can go off on our own and seek success. He has given it to us so that we will discover the purposes and plans he has designed for us. He has placed in us passions and aspirations that encourage us to pursue his purposes and bring him glory as he graciously uses us to expand his kingdom. The more we allow our passions and aspirations to pull us in the direction of God's sovereign plans for us, the more frequently we will enjoy the serenity and fulfillment for which we have been created. But during those times when we are determined to pursue our own definition of success, at the expense of God's plans for us, we, like Ginger, will experience the pain and frustration that very often result from fighting against God's will.

Holding Our Dreams Loosely

I am convinced the Bible teaches that God has a purpose for bringing each and every one of us into existence. He didn't give us life to just sit back and watch us wildly thrash around like a trout out of water, desperate to find our rightful place in his creation on our own. As I have said, our drive for success and our passion to achieve greatness are not inherently bad. Much to the contrary I believe they are indeed divine. God does not ask us nor does he want us to deny or sublimate our passions and desire for success. We should work diligently and with excellence toward achieving that to which we feel called. What is essential in this process, however, is that we hold our dreams, aspirations, plans, and visions loosely. It is vital that we be willing to allow our ambition and desire for success to be fulfilled in God's way and in his time.

We must accept the reality that the final outcome God has in mind for us may not look exactly like what we have envisioned for ourselves. But God's outcomes most certainly will be better for us and more fulfilling than anything we could have possibly achieved in our own ingenuity and strength.

Can we still dream? Absolutely! Should we still strive for excellence and effectiveness in all we do? We must;

we represent the King of the universe! Can we continue to plan aggressively for the future? Yes! But ultimately we do not insist that God meet our timetable and deliver the goods as we have ordered. We allow God to give direction and shape to our dreams and plans. As we release our personal plans and aspirations into his sovereign care, we will find a measure of serenity in ministry previously unknown to us and we will allow the fruit of our labors to be determined by God alone.

When we fail or refuse to hold our plans loosely and ultimately choose not to give them over to God, the results can be extremely frustrating and even destructive for both us and the church or organization we serve.

Far too many churches have been mortally wounded by a pastor or leader who insisted that his plans be implemented so that he could realize his personal dream when the time was not right and the people ill-prepared.

I have found that during those times when I have willfully forged ahead with my own plans and forced my personal agenda in ways that felt premature and awkward, I have always made a mess of the situation. Not that my plan was ungodly or my dream entirely misguided, it's just that it was not God's time.

Seeking God's Outcome

It is important for me to say once again that I am not in any way suggesting that we should simply slack off in ministry under the guise of letting God be God. Understanding the reality of God's sovereignty as it relates to our desires for personal success does not mean that we shouldn't employ the best in church growth technology and do everything as excellently as is possible with the resources God has given us.

But in the final analysis it does mean that we recognize God is sovereign in all of these efforts and that the outcomes will not always be what we had hoped or planned for them to be. It means that when we are not seeing the type of growth or the pace of change that we have planned for, we do not feel like a failure and become frustrated with the lack of visible progress.

Just because our church is not growing at the rate we have planned for does not mean God is displeased with us or that we have somehow missed his will. Even though we may not ever attain megachurch status in our ministry or write a best-seller that revolutionizes the Christian community, we can still find serenity and fulfillment in our ministry when we make peace with this paradoxical tension that exists between our need for personal success and the sovereign actions of God.

We can actually begin to enjoy this amazing journey that is ministry, regardless of the size of our church or how wide our popularity, when we finally allow ourselves to rest in the sovereign movements of God. After all, it is his church. No one desires the success of the church more than God does! So let's let him be the God not only of his church but of our life as well. We work hard. We keep our passion and desire alive. But we also allow God to take our church and us to the place where he wants us to be and on his timetable.

For some leaders, releasing their dreams of a megachurch and the national attention that so often accompanies such ministry success will be so difficult that they will continue to push ahead and even manipulate their churches in order to realize their personal dream. As mentioned earlier, when that happens, there will be a high price to pay and the currency in which it is paid will be frustration, anger, burnout, depression, and a whole host of other maladies that will make ministry miserable.

In chapter 4 I will diagnose these megachurch maladies in the hope that being forewarned will enable us to be forearmed. If we understand the costs of resisting God's sovereignty in favor of pursuing our own personal success, perhaps we will think twice before we have to actually pay the price.

Suggestions for Self-Reflection

1. How does the world around us measure success? How does the evangelical church world measure success (be honest now!)? How do you measure your own personal success?
2. Would you say that you are successful at the present time
    —personally?
    —spiritually?
    —financially?
    —professionally?
    —relationally?
    Why or why not?
3. Have you ever found yourself subtly yearning for spiritual celebrity status? Have you ever wished that someone would ask you to speak at a national event in an area of your expertise and success? Explore the significance of your answer—what does it tell you about yourself?
4. What does a successful church look like to you? What does a successful pastor look like to you? Do you really believe what you just wrote?
5. How would you react to the following statement: "If you work hard enough and smart enough, you are capable of creating a truly successful ministry"? Explain your response to this statement and be able to support it biblically.

6. What do you think success looks like from God's perspective?
7. How do you personally resolve the paradox of the need to make plans for church growth and effectiveness while at the same time embracing the sovereignty of God?
8. In what ways have you struggled with pursuing your own personal success while embracing the sovereignty of God? (Reflect on Psalm 139:16.)

FOUR

Success Sickness

When We Insist on Ministry Success

In Sebastian Junger's best-selling book *The Perfect Storm*, the tragic and true story of the commercial fishing vessel *Andrea Gail* is told in heartrending detail. The tale is in fact a parable of the steep price one man is willing to pay in pursuit of personal success.

Billy Tyne was a lifelong fisherman and the captain of the ill-fated *Andrea Gail*. As the story unfolds, it becomes clear that Billy is a man desperately in search of himself. He is looking for something that will give his life a measure of significance and in turn affirm his value and worth as a person. Because all he knows is the life of a Gloucester swordfisherman, he turns to the sea to find the success he hopes will satisfy the ache deep in his soul.

Throughout the book Billy and his crew are consistently outfished by the other boats of Gloucester. Eventually the continued survival of the *Andrea Gail*'s crew is threatened by their constant underachievement. Of course this simply reinforces the already negative image

Billy has of himself and intensifies his search for success and significance.

Finally, Billy makes a bold decision to head for the rich fishing grounds known as the Flemish Cap that lie off the outer banks of Newfoundland—an area made dangerous by its unpredictably severe weather and distance from the mainland. Because it is so late in the season, his plan to fish the Flemish Cap is an even more perilous decision. But Billy needs to score big in a short period of time if he is going to assuage his need for success and restore his sense of personal worth. So, in spite of warnings to reconsider, Billy sets off for the Cap in search of swordfish.

At their first fishing stop en route to the Cap, Billy and the crew strike out yet again, elevating the anger and frustration level of the crew. Billy is filled with self-doubt, and his crew begins to question his ability to find fish any longer and suggests that he has lost his touch—maybe it's time for him to hang up his hooks. As near mutiny breaks out aboard the *Andrea Gail*, Billy redoubles his determination to find fish. They will continue on to the Flemish Cap, Billy decides.

As the boat steams toward Billy's destiny, the fax machine in the wheelhouse begins to spit out ominous warnings of a major storm that is threatening the area, but Billy is so obsessed with his plan to find fish that he never notices the initial warnings. As they get closer to the fishing grounds, the weather advisories become increasingly dire, but now they are so close to the Cap that Billy cannot bear the thought of leaving for home empty-handed, in spite of the significantly increased danger to him and his crew.

Finally, the *Andrea Gail* and her crew reach the waters off the Grand Banks, set their lines, and wait. After much anxiety and with a sense of dread, Billy gives the order, "Let's fish, boys!" As they pull in their lines, huge, thrashing swordfish greet them. Never before have they seen so many fish at one time! The boat is scarcely able to contain the multitude of fish that they continue pulling in. With every swordfish brought onboard Billy finds a measure of success and vindication—maybe he is a person of value and worth after all.

In the midst of their fishing frenzy the fax machine continues to print out warnings of what has by this time become a hurricane that is on a course that will shortly place it directly between Billy's boat and the mainland. If they head for home immediately they will probably be able to beat the storm and return to Gloucester alive. After taking the risk and finally finding the fish, Billy refuses to leave without his catch—he would rather die.

Ultimately Billy gets his fish, filling the *Andrea Gail's* hold to overflowing. In fact they stuffed their boat with so many swordfish that the ancient ice machine could not handle the load and broke down. They would have to get to Gloucester in a hurry to salvage their catch.

Unfortunately, the hurricane had now positioned itself between the *Andrea Gail* and the mainland. Getting home with their fish would require them to steam right through the middle of the worst hurricane in one hundred years—the perfect storm. Because they had delayed their return for so long in an effort to get all of the fish they possibly could, their chances of survival were greatly diminished.

Billy's desperate need for success and personal affirmation had caused him to recklessly forge ahead in his quest for fish, ultimately resulting in the loss of the *Andrea Gail* and her entire crew—with her hold full of fish. Although he found the fish for which he had been so desperate, Billy's search for success was extremely costly, not only to him but also to the people around him. For Billy the pursuit of success at all costs ended in ultimate failure.

Ministry Success at All Costs

Like Billy there are many pastors and church leaders who are so desperate to realize ministry success and the personal affirmation they hope it will provide that they are willing to forge ahead with their plans and strategies at all costs. Though this drive is often cloaked in the goal of reaching the lost and advancing God's kingdom, all too frequently it is motivated more by the leader's need to feel successful and affirmed than it is by any altruistic ministry objectives.

When leaders attempt to build a big church and attract more numbers in an effort to gain success and feel good about themselves, it seems no price is too high. And many times the price that is paid in the pursuit of church-growth success is devastating not only to the leader but also to everyone around the leader.

Now I can imagine the inner resistance that is being felt by many reading these words and can almost hear the mental arguments that are forming to refute my assertion that the reckless pursuit of church growth can be extremely costly. But the reality is, if we are honest with ourselves, we are well aware of the fine line that exists between self-serving ministry efforts and the pure desire to advance God's kingdom. We have all fought the inner battle that rages when we desire ministry success and personal significance but sense that our plans and strategies may not be what God has in mind for us or the church to which he has called us. In fact at one time or another I am sure most of us have also been forced to experience the pain and fallout that result from forging ahead with our own plans and failing to listen to the inner prompting of the Holy Spirit.

When we recklessly pursue church growth at any price, we need to recognize that the price may prove to be even higher than we had anticipated. We may discover that not only is there an individual price to pay for such self-serving ministry efforts, there is also an enormous corporate cost as well.

Corporate Success Sickness

While I was attending seminary in southern California, there was a church in my neighborhood that was struggling to compete with some of the more rapidly growing churches in our area. The pastor of that church was an extremely gifted preacher who was also a popular leader in local church circles. The only trouble was that the church he pastored was not growing—at least not growing as fast or to the extent he thought that it should.

In an effort to jump-start some growth, he challenged the church to undertake a building project that would provide them with a more prominent and attractive sanctuary—something the pastor felt sure would attract new attendees, resulting in the much desired church growth.

During the campaign conducted by the pastor to convince the congregation that a new sanctuary was the key to their future growth, many members argued that the church could not afford to pay for the proposed building. If they did enter such a building project, they would have to borrow the money and most people within the congregation knew that they could not make the payments on such a loan if their giving remained static.

In response, the pastor explained that the building would be paid for with the help of those who joined the church as the result of the new sanctuary. Though things would be tight to begin with, the pastor conceded, it wouldn't be long before the new facility attracted enough new attendees to help foot the bill.

73

This pastor was so desperate to see his church grow as rapidly as others in the area were growing that he was even willing to take a significant financial risk in the hope of seeing success.

After a somewhat rancorous process, the church voted by a slim margin to undertake the building program. The construction project was eventually completed and the church opened its new sanctuary with much fanfare and celebration. The congregation hosted a series of open houses to attract visitors but they could get few of the newcomers to stick.

Next they produced several special events, again as a way to draw potential church members to their new sanctuary. Unfortunately, in spite of their best efforts, they were unable to gain many new members, and it wasn't long before the congregation began to feel the financial pinch that resulted from the heavy debt they were now servicing. Board members began getting nervous and the pastor struggled to understand why their beautiful new facility was not attracting new attendees as he felt sure it would.

Within a year after constructing the new building, the church was on the ropes financially and fighting for its life. Several key families departed in anger and others began to withhold their giving in protest. Eventually, just a couple of years after completing the project, the pastor left the church feeling defeated and frustrated. His plan to grow the church did not work and instead created a serious mess for that congregation.

By the time I completed my seminary studies, the church was a mere shell of what it had been when I moved into the area. To my knowledge the church still has not fully recovered from that desperate attempt to produce successful church growth.

Sadly the story of that church in southern California can be told of countless other churches across America.

Chances are you can name one or more churches that have been forced to endure a similar experience.

So what exactly does it cost a local church when those of us in ministry and spiritual leadership positions pursue church growth at any price? The cost can be measured on many different levels. Very often the scars resulting from a reckless pursuit of growth are not tangible; they can't always be quantified in dollars and cents or seen in church splits, but they can be devastating nonetheless. In addition to any intangible costs, when the attempt at transforming a church into the next megachurch of national renown fails, there is often a very tangible price tag as well.

What price might the church we serve be forced to pay as a result of our neurotic needs for success and self-affirmation? How might our efforts at self-promotion under the guise of church growth impact the local body we serve in the years that will follow our failed attempts? I think it is vitally important that we take some time to examine the potential pain and corporate costs we might inflict on those we leave behind when we take off after a failed attempt at church growth. The costs to a congregation can involve such things as a corporate sense of depression, congregational decline and potential division, crippling debt, and eventually even the death of a congregation.

Corporate Depression

All too often a pastor's failed attempt at church growth precipitates the onset of what can only be described as "corporate depression." Now, obviously, anytime a church loses a pastor, if the leader was loved at all, there will be a natural period of mourning and discouragement. But when a pastor leaves as the result of failed attempts at growth, even though that is not given as the reason for the resignation, the church will often experience a more pronounced form of corporate grief that goes well beyond that which is considered normal.

Many churches that have been unable to produce the numerical growth so desired by a pastoral administration slip into a period of depression after that pastor leaves the church. The leaders that are left behind feel discouraged because they were not able to deliver the church growth the pastor wanted and they begin to doubt their leadership ability and question whether they should be in leadership at all.

As the leadership begins to doubt and question themselves, their sense of failure begins to bleed into the corporate culture of the organization and the people of the congregation often begin to feel that they too are somehow to blame for the failed attempts at church growth. If they had been more spiritual or more committed to God, maybe the church would have grown and the pastor would have stayed. Even if they were not enthusiastic supporters of the pastor's growth plans, people have difficulty dealing with the fact that they were unsuccessful in meeting the pastor's goals.

I have been in many churches where there is an almost palpable sense of corporate depression. In these churches it is clear that the people have a very low self-image as a group and that they view their church as a failure. They wonder if any other pastor will want to come and give them leadership in the future, which obviously creates a very negative corporate environment. I have even consulted one church where the leaders and search committee articulated their feeling that they did not deserve another pastor because of their past failures at producing church growth. In fact this corporate depression, along with the feelings of unworthiness that it spawns, can easily create a form of self-fulfilling prophecy that actually scares potential pastors away from the church.

If the church does not recover from this sense of corporate depression within a reasonable period of time, they will experience another aspect of corporate success sickness—the church will begin to experience a significant decline in membership.

Congregational Decline

When a church is unable to recover from the feelings of failure and a poor corporate self-image created by failed attempts at growth and the loss of a pastor, it is easy for the church to enter a period of decline.

A church in the Midwest I am very familiar with experienced just such a cycle after the departure of a pastor who had been with them for more than ten years. During the first few years of his administration, this pastor was content with managing the status quo and keeping the deacons happy. Then, about midway into his tenure there, he attended a seminar by a well-known leadership figure who promoted a formulaic approach to church growth. This national leader inferred that numerical growth was the primary sign of effective leadership and that a failure to grow was a clear sign of ineffective leadership.

Stoked up by this conference the pastor returned to his congregation with a new zeal to see church growth and significant ministry expansion. Of course after his five years of serving primarily as a caretaker, the deacon board was shocked, to say the least, at their pastor's overnight metamorphosis into a take-no-prisoners leader.

Reenergized, the pastor quickly began to develop a three-year growth plan that he felt confident would rouse his sleeping flock into an on-fire army of spiritual soldiers ready to take their community for Christ. The first stage of the plan was a major renovation of their dated sanctuary in preparation for the influx of new people he knew would result from their efforts. The sanctuary makeover would require a fund-raising project, an effort that would also be used to raise funds for a major outreach thrust into the community.

After much intense effort the church successfully raised the needed funds and completed the renovation of their worship center. They organized and conducted a significant outreach into the community. However, the results of the outreach were not nearly what the pastor had hoped for, nor were they close to the projections he had used when motivating the board and congregation to enter into the three-year plan in the first place. Less than one year after the disappointing outreach attempt, the pastor was forced to resign by a disgruntled deacon board.

Because the deacon board did not conduct itself in a spiritual manner during the removal of the pastor, his dismissal created some hard feelings within the congregation. The pastor left under a cloud of disappointment and failure, though the board attempted to paint a happy face on all of the public activities related to his departure. Not long after the pastor's abrupt departure there was disagreement among the board members regarding the manner in which the removal was effected, resulting in several influential deacons leaving the board and the church.

The church entered into a period of corporate depression as a result of what appeared to be their massive congregational failure. The corporate depression deepened and spread to most members of the church. After more than a year and a half of deepening depression, the congregation began to experience substantial decline in numbers, staff, and ministry.

Today that church is literally hanging on by its corporate fingernails. At the time the pastor was forced to leave, the church's attendance had hovered around the 350 mark for morning worship. Previous to the pastor's leaving, the church employed four full-time staff members and offered a growing menu of ministry programs and opportunities. But, just two years after his abrupt departure, the church is now struggling to maintain even one hundred people in Sunday morning worship attendance. The entire staff has departed and the programs have declined to bare maintenance mode. If something significant does not interrupt the downward spiral of this church, it is likely to become another victim of acute corporate success sickness, as the decline leads to congregational death. Though the church had been stable and relatively healthy before this episode, the desire to see rapid church growth in an unrealistic time frame created corporate depression that eventually led to corporate decline on a dangerous scale.

While the pastor is to be admired and commended for his desire to make the transition from a spiritual caretaker to a more transformational leader, less emphasis on immediate numerical growth in favor of a more realistic and gradual transformation process may have prevented the tragic debacle that eventually occurred.

All too often in such cases, the destructive results of success sickness do not end with just congregational decline but escalate to the point of congregational division.

Congregational Division

When a church leader becomes intent on pursuing ministry success at any cost in the hope of producing significant and rapid church growth, one of the more frequent consequences can be an intrachurch division or even a formal church split.

These church divisions and splits are most often created by a difference in ministry philosophy among pre-existing factions within the church. In every church there seems to be a contingent among the congregation that believes the church's mission should be discipleship or the edification of believers. "We must disciple and develop the believers we already have before we try to reach more," is the mantra of this group.

At the same time there is another contingent within the congregation that believes the church's mission should focus on reaching the lost. The cry of this faction is, "At least the believers we already have are on their way to heaven! What about those who are eternally lost without Christ—we must reach them with the gospel!"

The pastors who desire to see rapid church growth most naturally cater to the evangelistically enthused segment of the congregation, causing the group committed to discipling to feel disenfranchised and ignored. The discipling contingent begins to feel that everything in the church is geared toward reaching new people and they ask, "What about us?" If the leadership does not adequately address these competing ministry philosophies, providing a unified and balanced ministry approach, the differences can lead to a significant corporate division.

According to Mark Mittleberg, author of *Building a Contagious Church*, the key to becoming what has been termed a "prevailing church" is the leadership's ability to fuse both of these competing ministry philosophies into a single, coherent philosophy that fuels both elements equally.[1] In fact it is a well-balanced ministry involving both areas that creates a prevailing church. But such a fusion is not easily fashioned. It requires prayer, patience, and modeling. It requires giving time to allow the new ministry philosophy to permeate every aspect of the church culture. Most advocates of church change suggest that such congregational change requires a minimum of four years to accomplish.[2]

When the leadership forges ahead with their outreach efforts without addressing the concerns of those who would focus on edification, the chasm between the two groups can develop into a polarizing division. If this division is allowed to deepen it has the potential of growing into a church split.

New Hope Church experienced just such a division and refused to deal with it patiently. Rather than taking the time necessary to forge a united ministry philosophy that recognized the importance of both evangelism and edification, a group within the congregation, led by a pastoral staff member desperate to see numerical growth, decided to splinter off and begin a "church plant." As is common in churches with internal struggles, the church leadership attempted to present the splinter group in a positive light, but everyone in the congregation knew what was actually happening. The church went ahead with the controlled church split, leaving many wounded and spiritually damaged people on both sides.

Within two years after the church-planting group began their efforts under the leadership of the pastor desperate to see growth, the church experienced what could only be called phenomenal growth. This group that began with little more than one hundred members grew to eighteen hundred! Unfortunately, the new church could not support such rapid growth. The swift increase in numbers outstripped the church's ability to manage what was taking place.

The leaders began to feel stressed in the areas of infrastructure, finances, facilities, and staff. Within little

81

more than two years the pastor left under pressure and less than healthy circumstances, throwing that growing new church into corporate depression and decline.

The church quickly recruited a new pastor who lasted little more than one year. The next pastor experienced a moral failure after just three years of ministry there. Today, just seven years later, that church plant has folded and closed its doors permanently.

Though a positive spin had been put on what was actually an unhealthy division within the congregation, no amount of spin could save the new congregation from this manifestation of success sickness and salvage the church.

Crippling Debt

Another form of success sickness that can infect a local congregation when a leader insists on seeing rapid growth and ministry expansion is the creation of un-healthy amounts of debt. In an effort to stimulate church growth, leaders are often too quick to rationalize and justify incurring large financial debt.

As in the example provided earlier in this chapter, far too many churches encumber themselves with unhealthy amounts of debt in an effort to finance new facilities that they hope will attract new attendees. Debt is often unwisely used to fund new staff positions or additional ministry programs with an eye toward producing numerical growth. In fact some churches even take on debt as a way to fund outreach events that they hope will eventually produce enough growth to service the debt.

The sad reality is that many churches are shackled with crippling debt that eventually stifles church growth and siphons money away from ministry programs and staff. I am aware of numerous churches that are currently servicing a disabling amount of debt as the result of a pastor's promotion of some creative plan to help their church grow, a plan that failed. Not only are those churches now laboring under a heavy load of financial debt, they also have never experienced the church growth the debt was supposed to fund. To exacerbate their problems, the pastor who encouraged the debt has moved on to another church, and the debt-ridden church is without a pastor.

Unhealthy debt is a symptom of success sickness that has crippled more than one local church.

Congregational Death

Ultimately, when a leader uses church growth as a vehicle to realize personal ministry success, there can be consequences even more serious than those already mentioned. In extreme cases the unhealthy pursuit of church growth and ministry success in an effort to massage a leader's neurotic ego needs can result in the death of a church. Without giving it much thought I can list three churches that have disbanded as a direct result of the reckless and unhealthy pursuit of church growth.

Not only are there heavy corporate costs that churches must pay as a result of a leader's selfish pursuit of church growth, there can also be a serious personal price exacted from the leader who perpetrates such spiritual malpractice.

Personal Success Sickness

When leaders insist on what they deem to be measurable ministry success, not only can the church as an organization experience negative effects but the leaders can also experience some painful personal consequences. When church growth doesn't come and success in ministry proves elusive, many leaders can experience an acute sense of discouragement and disappointment, feelings of personal failure, and anger directed toward the congregation. They may decide on premature resignation and even the eventual departure from ministry altogether.

Discouragement and Disappointment

Today there is more discouragement and disappointment among the ranks of spiritual leaders than many people realize. When a pastor works hard at producing tangible signs of growth and is obsessively concerned with whether or not the ministry is "successful," it can and often does lead to a sense of disappointment and a discouragement that borders on depression. When, like sea captain Billy Tyne, we can feel good about ourselves only when we see measurable signs of success, and that success never seems to come, it is a serious emotional blow that cripples us in our ministry efforts.

Unfortunately, one of the principal reasons for the escalating number of clergy members who are experiencing serious depression is the perceived inability to produce success in their ministry. It is vitally important that we as spiritual leaders recognize that we can do our very best and in fact be doing everything right and still not realize the growth and ministry expansion for which we long. When our emotional and spiritual well-being become inordinately dependent on the growth of our ministry rather than on who we are in Christ, the imbalance can create for us serious emotional problems.

84

A Sense of Failure

Another symptom of personal success sickness that is closely related to depression and disappointment is a sense of personal failure. When a pastor is unable to produce what he or she feels is adequate success in ministry, it can lead to a deep sense of personal failure.

As we have seen, in today's church culture where such a high value is placed on the megachurch and other rapidly expanding ministries, it is easy for leaders to feel that they are failing if they are unable to replicate in some way the success of these prominent, benchmark churches.

For many pastors today the failure to engineer noticeable ministry growth is a sure sign of personal failure—a sense of failure that often becomes debilitating.

Anger Directed toward the Church

A still more dangerous symptom of leaders suffering from success sickness is when a subtle anger toward their congregation begins to develop, affecting their life and ministry.

When leaders desperately need to experience success to feel good about who they are, and that success is not forthcoming, they can begin to project the failure onto the congregation in the form of anger. There are many pastors today who have begun to harbor anger and bitterness toward the congregation they serve because they feel that the congregation has in some way, whether intentionally or unintentionally, blocked their efforts at producing church growth.

When this anger begins to develop, it is often given expression publicly through harsh sermons and insensitive statements that begin to poison the relationship between pastor and people. Once this destructive process

85

has taken root, it is extremely difficult to restore the relationship between pastor and people. If allowed to continue, this misplaced anger and frustration will result in serious congregational dysfunction and ill health.

Premature Resignation and Ministry Dropout

Finally, one of the most devastating results of success sickness among clergy is their premature resignation from a ministry post or, ultimately, the departure from ministry altogether. When pastors begin leaving ministry positions too soon, simply because they do not see the degree of growth they desire as quickly as they would like, it can begin to establish a very negative pattern in their life and ministry. The danger is that regardless of where they are, when things don't happen on their timetable they are too quick to leave, seeing it as a ministry failure.

Percy C. Ainsworth, a nineteenth-century British pastor, put it this way:

> Some people have only one suggestion to offer when they have failed: "We will try somewhere else." Because they have caught nothing [produced no significant growth] they conclude that there is nothing to catch. That logic afflicts not only the self-inflated and the impatient, but all of us now and again. Perhaps it is only natural that we dream of better work in a new field.[3]

The reality is that God may want to teach the leader something that can be taught only through not allowing the church to grow for a season. By quitting too soon, the pastor misses out on the blessings that God intended and the ultimate fruit that will result from such a "fallow" season of ministry. And after a string of these aborted attempts at producing church growth, it is all too common for pastors to conclude that God must not have called them to ministry or that they are not gifted for the task. But closer to the truth is the fact that God has been more concerned with the minister's own personal and spiritual growth during this time than he has been with the growth of the churches he has been called to serve. The church growth will always come in due course when the minister has been shaped and formed by the Chief Gardener. But all too often one of the shapes personal success sickness takes is premature resignation and ministry dropout.

When Success Comes Too Fast

Today it seems that anyone who has an extra sixty-five thousand dollars lying around feels they have got to climb Mount Everest. In recent years the number of people attempting to scale the world's highest peak has exponentially multiplied. Most of these people are weekend warriors who want to spice up their middle-aged life with some high adventure that is beyond the ordinary.

Unfortunately, climbing mountains like Everest takes more time than many are willing to invest. There is a tendency for these recreational climbers to ascend the mountain too quickly. Rather than spend the long weeks necessary to properly acclimate themselves to this life-threatening environment, they would much rather "just do it."

But when you try to succeed too quickly in the Himalayas, you are inviting tragedy. For climbers who ascend too fast, there is a high likelihood that they will be overcome by high altitude pulmonary edema (known as HAPE) or high altitude cerebral edema (commonly called HACE), two serious ailments that are deadly if immediate action is not taken. On virtually every expedition to Everest, as well as to the other eight-thousand-meter peaks of the world, more than one climber will be overcome and immobilized by one or both of these altitude-induced ills.

What happens when we are successful at producing church growth but it comes too rapidly? Is it always a good thing to see exponential growth in a local church, or is it possible that even when we are successful at producing numerical growth, it can have a negative or even destructive impact on the health and life of the church?

The reality is that when church growth comes too fast, it can create significant challenges. That is not to say they are insurmountable challenges, but they are, nonetheless, challenges that can shake the foundations of a church as well as the inner foundations of those who give the church leadership.

During the rapid, supernatural expansion of the New Testament church, recorded in the Book of Acts, we can see some of the problems created when a church grows quickly. In Acts 6 we can see that even though God was the obvious author of this miraculous church growth, the apostles faced a serious potential crisis that threatened the unity of the church because the church was experiencing rapid growth in a short span of time.

One of the challenges that rapid church growth and ministry expansion will create involves outgrowing the church's infrastructure, which provides for the adequate governance and support systems necessary for a healthy church.

Another challenge will be the increased need for godly, spiritually mature leaders. In my church-planting experience one of the greatest challenges I faced was the need for qualified leaders who could keep pace with the rapid growth of the congregation. There are few things that will create more serious problems in the local church than placing people in leadership positions when they are not spiritually or emotionally equipped to fill those positions.

Yet another serious challenge when rapid ministry expansion is experienced is the need for appropriate physical facilities. We often reason that substantial church growth will result in an inevitable increase in the financial resources of the church. But that generally is not the case. When growth comes too fast, the product of aggressive efforts to attract newcomers, the people we attract are very often not spiritually or emotionally prepared to immediately contribute financially to the ministry of the church.

More often than not, these new attendees become a drain on the already limited financial resources of the local church before they ever begin to give in any substantial and methodical manner. The result is that the church must now expand existing ministries to provide for a larger number of people, while at the same time the financial resources remain the same. This can place even the most healthy church in a temporary economic bind that often results in increased leadership stress levels and more aggressive competition among staff and ministry departments for limited resources.

Another result of rapid spikes in attendance can be an increased usage of many products that cannot be recycled. Things such as crayons in the children's department and Sunday school curriculum materials are found to be in short supply. The production of worship bulletins and information pieces requires more paper, more toner, not to mention more labor to put all these materials together.

A large influx of new people places increased pressure on the physical plant that can also be costly. Often overlooked in this area are the increased costs to cool or heat the facility due to the larger number of bodies

89

in the building. There is greater wear and tear on floor coverings, and inadequate furniture in education spaces becomes an issue that must be dealt with. The rapid infusion of new people requires a greater number of chairs, tables, classrooms, and other physical necessities.

There are many areas in the life of the church that will be dramatically impacted by a sudden increase in numbers. But all too often these issues are never considered by those planning and promoting the outreach activities. As leaders, we are prone to reason that God will provide the resources if the people are brought in.

Now obviously God can provide for the needs of his church. However, we need to make sure we are giving sufficient attention to these important matters prior to our efforts to increase attendance. The problems I have personally experienced, as well as those I have observed secondhand in this area, generally occurred when the numerical growth was pursued for growth's sake as opposed to when God is at work bringing more manageable growth. Such was the case with New Hope Church, which I mentioned on pages 81 and 82.

Sacrificing Success for the Corporate Good

During the time that I was completing this chapter, the nation was thrown into a political purgatory when the result of the presidential election of 2000 was too close to call even one month after the voting took place. Day after day the country was subjected to a series of press conferences and increasingly combative statements as both the Bush and Gore campaigns ratcheted up the rhetoric in attempts to secure ultimate victory.

After two recounts of the vote in Florida, the state that was the key to victory for both candidates, Governor George W. Bush was determined to have garnered the most votes, thus winning that state's twenty-five electoral college votes and, as a result, the presidency.

However, in spite of the recounts confirming Governor Bush's triumph in Florida, Vice President Al Gore refused to concede the election. Instead, the vice president proceeded to drag the country through a prolonged process of litigation in an attempt to snatch victory from the jaws of defeat.

Commenting on what could possibly motivate a leader of such stature to pursue personal victory and success at the expense of the national interest, Andrea Mitchell of MSNBC stated, "When you have spent your entire life preparing to be the president, it is hard to let go."[4]

By all accounts the vice president had set his sights on the presidency at an early age—it had become a personal obsession. In fact most observers and biographers of his life believe that Al Gore had been groomed for ascendancy to the highest office in the land by his parents from the beginning of his life.[5] Because it was a lifelong goal, losing such a close race for the presidency was very hard to accept. As a result the vice president seemed only too willing to pursue a course of action that would be detrimental to the entire country in an effort to realize the personal success that he had dreamed of for so long. Senator Bob Kerry of Nebraska put it this way, "In a campaign it is easy to feel that the ends justify the means—in the current situation [the wrangling over recounts and the threats of litigation] that attitude could be very costly to the nation."[6]

Rather than looking out for what was best for the nation, even if it meant that he would not realize a personal dream, the vice president was willing to drag the nation through a very painful experience that may have established some very unhealthy precedents for future close elections.

91

Though the desire for personal success is often used by God in the life of the leader to keep him or her pressing forward through many different obstacles and challenges, there comes a time when the desire for personal success must take a backseat to the greater corporate good. Ted Koppel, speaking on the news program *Nightline,* said, "The fact is that both candidates are intensely competitive. After all, they didn't get to where they are without a strong drive for success. But at some point, sooner rather than later, one of them will have to put the good of the nation above their own desire to avoid personal failure."[7]

The same can be said of many well-intentioned pastors and church leaders. Though God has placed within them a desire to see the church grow and see people come to faith in Christ, they also have a primary responsibility to realize these desires in a way that advances the corporate good.

For pastors who struggle with feelings of personal inadequacy and failure, it means they must balance their need for personal ministry success against what is best for the church they serve. Rather than finding their worth and value in personal achievement and what they perceive to be success, it will mean finding a measure of transcendent significance in their relationship with Christ and the knowledge that they are being faithful to their calling.

Avoiding success sickness will require that we learn to entrust the results of our church and its growth to God, believing that he will always do what is best for his people and that he will ensure his kingdom continues to advance.

Again this does not in any way excuse us from hard work, strategic planning, purpose-driven leadership, striving for excellence, and doing all that we can to see that God's name is glorified in the work of his church.

But it does mean that we learn to trust him with our life and with the life of the church to which he has called us. I believe we will know that we are trusting God in this matter when we experience a sense of inner peace, confidence, and even serenity when all of our efforts fall short of what we had hoped for. When we are truly trusting God with our life and the life of our ministry, we will be able to minister with joy and hope because we know that God is in sovereign control of them both.

In the final analysis it is a lack of trust in the sovereign plan of God for our life and the life of the church that drives us to unhealthy attempts at producing growth. In the next chapter we will take time to understand the struggle we all face to trust in God's sovereignty and then we'll explore some of the fears that make it difficult for us to trust God with our life and our plans for the future. Learning how to trust God in this way will take us one step closer to finding a serenity in God's sovereignty that will enable us to recover a new measure of joy and delight in ministry and avoid experiencing the traumas of success sickness.

Suggestions for Self-Reflection

1. What are the forces most at work in your life that create your desire to see your church grow and experience what others will see as "success"? Is it really just a desire to see God's kingdom expanded, or are some of your human needs involved as well?
2. In what ways have you felt the need to produce substantial church growth in as short a time as possible? From where did this pressure come?
3. If you were to be very transparent, would you have to admit that there have been times when you succumbed to the desire to see rapid church growth?

How did it feel? What were the results—for you—for the church?

4. Have you been aware of churches that have experienced some (or all) of the costs associated with corporate success sickness? What were the costs? How could they have been avoided?

5. Why is it difficult to let go of the desire or dream of leading a church to rapid growth and pastoring a large church—even after years of failed attempts? Is that something that you struggle with? Why is there such a struggle?

6. In what ways have you experienced personal success sickness as described in this chapter? Could your bout with personal success sickness have been avoided? How?

FIVE

Letting Go of the Need to Succeed

Trusting God to Do What's Best

When she was five our daughter Hillary was faced with the exciting opportunity of spending three weeks alone with her grandma and grandpa in Spokane, Washington. As our two older children began telling Hillary how great Grandma's house was, we could see the look of desire in her eyes. Her brother and sister told her about a two-story Swiss chalet playhouse, complete with beds, sink, fridge, and stove. Grandma and Grandpa also had a huge jungle gym playground with swings and slides. There were bikes, roller skates, toys, and nights of pizza and movies at Grandma and Grandpa's house—a kid's paradise!

But even as Hillary considered the potential joys of Grandma's house, we could tell that she was afraid to leave the comfort of the known and familiar. After all, Spokane is a long way from Omaha, Nebraska, especially for a five-year-old.

Hillary was torn between two choices. She could choose to remain in the safety and predictability of the known and avoid the unknown, although it held the promise of adventure and excitement. Letting go of the known and what she felt comfortable with was a very difficult choice for Hillary to make. At least while she was at home with her mom and me, she felt that she was in control. She knew what would happen if she stayed home; the routine was familiar and without surprise. But allowing Grandma and Grandpa to take her to where she had never been before—a place that held unknown possibilities and where she felt out of control—that was an extremely difficult decision.

Finally, Hillary decided to trust her grandma and grandpa and she stepped out into the unknown for the scary journey to Spokane. Ultimately Hillary decided she had enough trust in her grandparents to know that they would not take her to a place that would not be good for her. She knew she could trust her older brother and sister and their descriptions of what awaited her at Grandma and Grandpa's house.

But I can still see Hillary's face, full of five-year-old apprehension, as Grandma and Grandpa's car pulled away from our house for the long and uncertain journey to Washington.

Not long after Hillary arrived in Spokane, she called home to inform us that Grandma and Grandpa's house was even better than Seth and Jill had told her. Hillary had stepped out in trust, she had given control of her life over to people who loved and cared for her more than she could know, and she ended up in a very happy place.

Letting Go for the Trip of a Lifetime

I am convinced that the primary reason we resist giving control of our life and destiny over to God is because we struggle with trust, as Hillary did. Though we intellectually believe that God loves us and that he desires to do only what is eternally best for us, it is difficult for us to release the reins of our life and allow him to take us where he will in this world.

We have ideas about what our life should look like and what we would like to accomplish during our lifetime, so we worry that if we let go completely of our personal life plan, God might take us where we don't want to go. As a result, we attempt to orchestrate the events of our life and career so that we ultimately arrive at the destination we have charted for ourselves. After all, following God can be dangerous business. What if he has a plan for our life that doesn't coincide with what we have planned? It just seems so much easier and safer to maintain the controls of our life and aggressively pursue the personal success and accomplishments for which we have spent our life preparing.

We recklessly pursue personal success in the local church context, even to the point of experiencing all sorts of corporate and personal success sickness, because the bottom-line truth of the matter is we find it difficult to trust God with our life. Sure, we preach about trusting God and are quick to encourage others to trust God to do only what is best for them, but functionally we live as if we are responsible for our ultimate destiny. We say that we believe in the sovereignty of God, but it is much more difficult to live out that belief in a world where competition and personal success rule the day. Because it is contrary to everything we have been taught in our culture, we find it exceedingly difficult to give our life and future over to an entity we cannot see. In our culture it is difficult, if not impossible, not to notice that it seems to be those who set deliberate goals and strategically direct their lives toward the realization of those goals who achieve what the world recognizes as great success.

From all outward appearances it seems to me that the people who are constantly plotting and planning, deal making, and scheming behind the scenes to advance themselves are the ones who actually do get ahead in life. The people who strategically plan each career move are the people who end up on top of their profession. As a result, the temptation is strong for those of us in ministry and spiritual leadership to plot out a career track and manage our life just as any other successful executive might do. We must remember, though, that a career is something we create ourselves; a calling is something we respond to and follow.

I remember a conversation I had years ago with a very gifted friend of mine who was also a pastor. We were both relatively young in ministry and filling our first senior positions in local churches. At the time, he was being considered for a much larger church that had significantly more visibility than his current ministry. As we talked, I asked him what he thought he might do about this new opportunity. I will never forget his response. Without batting an eye he said, "I'll probably accept the position, stay there for five to seven years, then move to a larger church for another five years or so. I figure after a couple of stints in a larger leadership venue, I'll be ready to assume the presidency of a Christian college or seminary." I didn't know quite how to respond. I remember how I bristled at what seemed to be such a cold and calculated view of ministry. This young pastor was intent on fulfilling his personal dream, and it seemed as if the churches he served were merely stepping-stones that enabled him to move further down the predetermined path he had laid out for himself. I remember wondering if he intended to share his career plans with this new church during the interview process. How would this church looking for a pastor feel about such plans?

I don't believe my friend is all that unique to those in ministry—he just happened to have the chutzpah to articulate it. The reality is that many of us in ministry and spiritual leadership struggle with the natural temptation to look at our ministry in much the same way.

Though we might find ourselves feeling uncomfortable with that kind of thinking when we become aware of it, most of us know only too well how easy it can be to fall into that trap—after all, how are we going to get ahead unless we take responsibility for our own future? How is our church going to grow and our ministry expand if we don't make it happen?

The Trouble with Trust

I must confess that this has been the most difficult chapter of this book for me to write because it expresses in many ways exactly where I find myself at the present time. Ironic, isn't it? While I am writing a book on finding serenity in God's sovereignty, I find myself struggling to find serenity in my own life and ministry. I suppose you might say that I am writing by faith, not by sight. My writing serves me as a tangible expression of my faith that God *is* in control of my life and that he *does* have a sovereign plan for my life, even though I am groping at present to find the express shape that it is supposed to take.

In my present state of professional groping and struggle, the key, I know, is learning to trust in God to the point that I can release my life into his sovereign care. I have got to resist the strong temptation to begin planning and plotting a path that will bring me increased recognition and material success. And believe me, the temptation becomes stronger with each passing year. The older we get, the more desperately we want to know

99

that we have accomplished something and that our life has made a difference.

Without wanting to sound self-aggrandizing or egoistic, I have to admit that I have a sense of destiny that has been planted deep within my soul—a sense that God has destined me to do something significant for him. It is a sense of destiny that dates back to when I was a young child. This sense of destiny is not uncommon to those of us called into spiritual leadership. In fact I am convinced, as is Dr. J. Robert Clinton, author of the now classic book *The Making of a Leader,* that this sense of destiny is one of the ways God processes and forms the people he has chosen for leadership in his church.[1] At times this sense of destiny gives me an almost palpable feeling that God wants to do something special in and through my life. It is a sense that causes me to persevere through the many hardships of ministry and keeps me putting one foot in front of the other on this journey called Christian service, in the hope that one day I will realize the full shape and detail of that for which God has destined me.

Because I have this inner sense of destiny, it is a constant temptation for me to connect the dots and fill in the blanks of my life all by myself. But every time I begin to charge ahead with my own plan for what my destiny should look like, I get a very unsettled feeling deep within my spirit. I find it difficult to fully explain this spiritual sensation in words. But suffice it to say that when I am moving ahead in my own strength, in an effort to advance my own personal plan and find my own success, it becomes absolutely crystal clear to me that I am usurping a role that belongs to God alone.

Recently, as I described briefly in chapter 3, I navigated through a period in my life when I desperately wanted to establish my own ministry of speaking and writing and transition to it as my full-time ministry. In many ways the new direction made sense. But the entire time I was planning the launch of this new endeavor, I had an unsettled feeling deep within my spirit. The reason for this gnawing feeling within me was that the launch of this new ministry was really more about me and my personal advancement than it was about God and the advancement of his kingdom. I wanted to create more speaking opportunities to sell more books and make more money. Even as I write these words, they leave a bad taste in my mouth and look ugly on the page. But they express the truth.

The same experience has all too often been true in my ministry as the pastor of a local church. On too many occasions I have advocated new directions and ministry programs to produce tangible signs of growth that I thought might eventually help to accelerate my ministry "career" (I use the word *career* advisedly only because that is how I and many others have tended to approach our service in the local church). Sure, I have always been careful to couch my intentions and plans in spiritual language that gives the perception that I am concerned with nothing but spiritual altruism, but the Lord has known those times when it was really more about me than it was about him.

The point of this extended confession is to draw attention to just how difficult it is for us to consistently trust God with our life and ministry. There is a razor-thin line that we in ministry must constantly walk if we are to be true to our calling and the sense of destiny God has planted deep within us. We cannot deny the transcendent sense of destiny we feel; it is always there, reminding us that there is something more for us in life and ministry.

However, at the same time, it is critical that we recognize that this sense of destiny has been given to us by God to motivate us for the work of ministry. It has not been given to us so that we can make a name for ourselves and use Christ's church as a platform for career advancement. It is a calling to make a kingdom difference that will transcend our life and bring glory to God, very often at the expense of our own ego and material benefit.

With that said, it must be recognized that there can be times when our faithfulness in the pursuit of God's calling produces as a natural by-product a degree of public recognition and even, possibly, material gain. But it is vital that we remember these benefits are a by-product, a sovereign serendipity (if such an oxymoron is possible), not the direct result of our planning and effort.

I am convinced that Christian leaders like Chuck Swindoll and Bill Hybels are very reluctant Christian celebrities. I do not believe they, or others like them, set out to create a name for themselves or to become the focus of national and international attention. I firmly believe that their fame is an unexpected result of their faithfulness to God's calling. They labored for years in anonymity, slugging it out in the ministry trenches just like many of us. They did not sit down at some point in their life and plot out how they could become international Christian leaders.

Bill Hybels tells of how he wrestled with God and resisted the calling to begin a local church. He did not have a seminary degree. He was not a dynamic speaker. He had no church leadership experience. He had his sights set on a career in the successful family business and was more interested in flying planes and sailing boats than he was in pastoral ministry. But ultimately, with fear, trembling, and tears, Bill relented and accepted God's call to enter what he felt sure would be a life of anonymous struggle as the young pastor of a new church start.

Like so many Christian leaders before and after him, Bill Hybels found success in life and ministry by trusting his life to the sovereign plan of God, in spite of his fears and misgivings. Again, it is important for us to be reminded at this point of how deceitful our hearts can be.

Some of us, desperate for personal success, may even be tempted to adapt this story as a formula for success and church growth. If we just "let go and let God," we reason, then we will realize success. It is amazing the degree to which we can deny our unhealthy, selfish motivations and allow our dark side to drive us from one ministry frustration to another.

Learning to trust God with our life and ministry is easier said than done, but I believe it is one of the most elementary and crucial thresholds through which we must pass before God will be able to bless us with an increased measure of ministry success and responsibility.

Those in Christian ministry who grasp for recognition and success are often denied it for the very reason that they need it too much; their success is more important to them than is God's ministry. Others, desperate for power and success, are allowed to achieve it temporarily, only to have it ripped away from them as the result of some shameful ministry failure, a sovereign lesson in character development that they would learn in no other way.

At times I wonder what it will take before I am able to entrust my life to God without caveat or reservation. How many times does God have to prove to me that "his ways are higher than my ways"? Why do I find it so difficult to realize that everything I have, all that I have achieved, and all of the victories I have experienced have been the result of God's sovereign work in my life? I can claim none of them. In fact there are times I can scarcely believe what God has made of my life and where he has

103

taken me. These things are not the result of some master plan I created or some series of tactical goals I dreamed up; they are the direct result of God's master plan for me.

My life, to this point, is a testimony to the truth of Psalm 139 where the psalmist writes in verse 16, "You saw me before I was born. Every day of my life was recorded in your book. *Every moment was laid out* before a single day had passed."[2] That can be the only explanation for what has taken place in my life. And the truth of that Scripture will also determine all that is yet to take place in my life.

In Ephesians 2:10 the apostle Paul says the same thing in another way. Paul says, "For we are God's masterpiece. He has created us anew in Christ Jesus, *so that* we can do the good things *he planned for us long ago.*" The Bible clearly teaches that God does have a plan for me, a plan that he specially designed for me from eternity past. That is the reason I have such a strong sense of destiny—he has given me a destiny!

You see, our role as Christian leaders is not to spend our energy manipulating and plotting ways that we can force church growth and advance ourselves in ministry. Our responsibility is not to lay out a master plan for our life that will lead us into a future of our own grandiose design. Our job is to trust God with our life. Our responsibility is to grip firmly the truth that God planned good things for us to do before we were ever born and then to invest our life in discovering what those things are. It means that we allow God's best to come to us rather than feeling as if we have to desperately chase after what we think we want and what we feel would be best for us. I am convinced that God is often just waiting for us to walk in reckless trust in him before he reveals the next segment of our destiny.

Early in my ministry I found it easier to trust God than I do now. Then there was not much to lose; life was full of possibilities with plenty of time to make mid-course corrections if things weren't working out. But with age comes the realization that we have a limited amount of time. At midlife, it hits us that if success and material blessings don't come soon, if they aren't just around the corner, they may never come. When we sense the clock winding down on our life, we know we don't have as much wiggle room and recovery time if things aren't happening the way we'd hoped. As a result, it is easy to feel a sense of desperation and begin forcing things in our pursuit of success and significance.

Since indeed the clock is winding down on our life, how much more essential it is that we recklessly entrust our lives to God, as opposed to wasting precious time manufacturing and pursuing our own feeble plans for self-advancement! If we truly want to realize our destiny and accomplish all of the good things God created for us to do before we were born, we will need to recover our ability to trust God completely with all of our life. He alone is able to bring his plans for us to fruition.

But how can we learn to let go of our life and future and give them over completely to the control and direction of God? What will it require before we can truly experience a consistent measure of contentment and serenity in our life and ministry? Is it possible to aggressively pursue positive ministry outcomes while at the same time maintaining a measure of inner tranquillity that promotes our spiritual well-being and that of the organization to which we give leadership? The answer to the last question is yes, but it will require that we learn and then master a trait that does not come naturally to those of us who strive for success and are driven by the need to achieve. We must learn to trust. More to the point, we will have to learn how to become almost reckless in our trust of God before we are able to find the serenity for which we seek.

Reckless Trust

Recovering a sense of serenity in God's sovereignty will require that we learn how to trust God completely, that we have an absolutely reckless trust in God.

To be reckless is to be wild and unconcerned with the consequences of an action. When we are living recklessly, we are careless and carefree. Reckless people engage in behavior that scares those who are more rational and sensible. I am proposing that we become people who are able to throw caution to the wind and trust God completely with our life and future. We must step out in trust to do things that most normal people would consider foolhardy and dangerous.

Of course a necessary prerequisite to such reckless trust is that we become resolutely convinced of God's incredible and amazing love for us as his children. We will need to be convinced that God will do only what is eternally best for us and that he is in the process of weaving even the most painful and evil circumstances of our life into an exquisite tapestry, the design of which was traced out by the hand of God from eternity past.

Before we are able to consistently rest in the sovereignty of God, we will need to embrace the reality that there is no personal plan we can achieve, and no destination at which we can arrive as a result of our own navigation, that can even begin to rival what God has in mind for us. Our relationship with God must be such that, when God needs us for a task or has an assignment for us, we are available to him and he is able to get our attention and communicate his plans to us.

It is not up to us to determine where we will go or what we will do in ministry. We are God's servants and we must submit our life to him. We must trust that he will use us when and where he deems we will be most effective at advancing his kingdom. We must be willing to learn the lessons that he needs us to learn so that we will be even more effective for future tasks and assignments. But if we refuse to learn the importance of recklessly trusting God with our life and ministry, we will be the ones who suffer the most—we may well miss out on God's best for us and have to temporarily settle for the second best of our own making.

Failure to Realize God's Best

One of the reasons that Israel constantly struggled under the discipline of God was their inability to trust him completely for their future in spite of his amazing provision and care for them.

In Deuteronomy 1:29–33, as Moses prepares to lead the people of Israel into the future God had promised them—a promise that had been delayed as a result of the people's lack of trust—he takes time to remind them why their forefathers did not realize God's greatest blessing:

> But I said to you, "Don't be afraid! The LORD your God is going before you. He will fight for you, just as you saw him do in Egypt. And you saw how the LORD your God cared for you again and again here in the wilderness, just as a father cares for his child. Now he has brought you to this place." But even after all he did, you refused to trust the LORD your God, who goes before you looking for the best places to camp, guiding you by a pillar of fire at night and a pillar of cloud by day.

107

Moses is reminding the people that it was the previous generation's refusal to trust God's sovereign care and provision for them that landed them in the wilderness for forty years.

Moses wants the people to understand that God has a plan for them; it's a plan that predates their existence and is independent of anything they have done or ever will do to merit it. God has a destiny for his chosen people and he wants them to realize all the fullness of that destiny. But that will require them to place absolute trust in God, even when it doesn't make human sense.

In this passage Moses communicates to the people that God is so intimately involved in the fulfillment of their divine future that he will actually go before them to find the best places for them to camp along the way. God is personally involved in leading the people into their destiny and will guide them daily by means that they can discern—a pillar of cloud by day and a pillar of fire by night. It is not for them to chart their own course. They do not have to determine their destination, because God has already taken care of the details of the journey himself. Their responsibility is to trust God and follow him with reckless abandon.

To realize God's best for them, the Israelites must develop spiritual discernment so that they can follow God's leading. They must become so close to God and so dependent on him that they are able to notice when he points them in a new direction or indicates that it is time to stop and camp. A failure to do these things will result in an aborted journey just as the previous generation experienced. Realizing God's best for them will require absolute trust.

The same is true for us. As we have already seen, God has a destiny for us. He created good things for us to do before we were even born. Our job is not to determine what we will do with our life or plan the shape our future will take. Our responsibility is to learn how to follow God so closely that we are able to discern his divine directions. We must learn how to recklessly follow God, even at those times when it might not make human sense, trusting that God will lead us only into his best for us. That is not to say that his best will always be easy or totally enjoyable. It does mean that it will be what is eternally best for us and in concert with his sovereign plan for our life.

Putting Trust to the Test

I remember when my wife, Sue, and I felt God calling us to go to seminary and prepare for ministry. God's leading was undeniable and unavoidable. He confirmed his direction for us in countless ways. We knew that God wanted us in seminary; the only decision for us was whether we would do what God wanted or what we wanted. That's how clear it was to us.

After much prayer and counsel we made the decision to attend Talbot School of Theology at Biola University in southern California. In preparation we put our house on the market, gave notice at our jobs, and began selling possessions that we couldn't afford to take with us. Miraculously God sold our house for the price we were asking—a true miracle in light of the double-digit interest rates of the early eighties. We quit our jobs and moved into the basement of my in-laws' house. We had a massive yard sale to liquidate most of our earthly treasure and made arrangements for hauling our remaining furniture and personal effects to the Golden State.

About a week before our scheduled departure from Spokane, Sue had a routine medical exam in an effort to wring every last penny of value from our soon-to-be-

109

lost health insurance. I will never forget the moment she returned from that checkup; the look on my wife's face is forever etched into my memory. After a brief hello she proceeded to inform me through a flood of uncontrollable tears that we were pregnant! She was almost two months along. Wow! What a life-changing surprise that little announcement was!

Here we were, certain God had called us to seminary. We had faithfully made all the preparations to follow him. We had no house. We had no jobs. We had no insurance and scarcely enough money to pay for the first year of seminary. I had planned on Sue's job as a waitress footing the rest of the seminary bill, but how in the world was she going to work as a waitress when in seven months she would give birth to our first child?

Suddenly the decision to attend seminary didn't seem quite as wise and reasonable as it had just a few days before. What in the world was God doing by jerking the proverbial rug out from under us? Why couldn't he have informed us of this little miracle just a month earlier, before we sold our house, quit our jobs, and were without insurance? It didn't make sense. Had we misunderstood God's direction in our lives? What would we do now?

God in his divine sovereignty put us in a position where we had only two options. We could trust God to provide for our considerable needs or we could fall back on our own ingenuity and schemes. It was at that moment that I learned the definition of trust. God had forced us to put to the test our trust in him.

Today, with the luxury of twenty years of hindsight, I realize that that episode was to be only the first of many opportunities to entrust our lives completely to God. It was God's way of creating an opportunity to demonstrate his utter trustworthiness at the beginning of our journey. If God could take care of us in this situation, surely

110

we could trust him with any other challenges we would face in the years of ministry to come.

God did not disappoint us. He miraculously provided health insurance that covered our preexisting pregnancy 100 percent. Through a truly serendipitous meeting, God provided Sue with a job, not as a waitress, but as a bank teller, a field in which she had absolutely no experience. She would be able to work right up until her due date. God provided me with a job at *Insight for Living*, the radio ministry of Chuck Swindoll, because it just so happened that I had experience with the exact type of IBM computer they were preparing to install in their data processing department. What a coincidence!

God put together a plan for us that we could have never even begun to duplicate in terms of its complexity and completeness. Not a single detail was left out. God's direction in our lives could not have been clearer had he provided us with pillars of cloud and fire. We had stepped out in absolute trust, willing to recklessly follow him, and he connected all of the dots and filled in all of the blanks—perfectly.

In the years since then God has never failed us. I have failed him. I have tried at times to orchestrate an instant version of his plan for my life, always to my own grief and frustration. But God has proven to me again and again that he is going before me, finding just the right places for me to exercise the gifts he has given me so that I can realize the plan he has for me. And yet, as I described at the beginning of this chapter, I still struggle periodically with letting go of my own personal plans and allowing God to direct me into the destiny he has for me.

There have been times too numerous to mention when I have attempted to manufacture church growth and ministry expansion in an effort to satisfy my own neurotic ego needs. During those times my plans have

111

almost always failed miserably and caused me to suffer depression and all other forms of success sickness.

Conversely, there have been times when I have been more intent on discerning God's direction, loving him completely, and glorifying him in my life and work above all else, absolutely oblivious to church growth tactics and techniques, and God has brought explosive growth— both numerical and spiritual.

Throughout my life and ministry, during those times when I have been most intent on simply being faithful to the call, God has taken me to places professionally that I had always hoped to go but had no idea how to get there. My first book was published without any effort on my part whatsoever. (Publishing a book was a dream that had long lain dormant, because I feared that it might never be realized.) A leadership formation ministry that I had attempted to give birth to on several occasions suddenly came together with very little planning when I finally turned it over to God. Today that ministry is expanding and flourishing with little energy from me—I find myself just trying to keep pace with what God is doing.

Over and over again God has proven that he can be trusted with my life and ministry. So why is it that I still struggle with letting go? What is it that causes me to attempt managing my own affairs and realizing my destiny under my own steam? Just because I know that the key to realizing my destiny is to trust God completely with my life doesn't mean that I have yet mastered the art of recklessly trusting God.

As it was for the children of Israel, it is most often our fear that keeps us from consistently trusting God with our future and finding the serenity in life and ministry for which we yearn. We struggle with a fear of the unknown, fear of loss, fear of unrealized dreams, and fear of failure. And before we are able to trust God, we need to face these fears and move beyond them.

The Fears That Make It Tough to Trust

Fear of the Unknown

One of the fears that can paralyze us when it comes to trusting God with our future is a fear of the unknown. If we let go of our well-devised plans and leave everything up to God, where might we end up and what might we find ourselves doing in the future? If we leave the future of our church in the hands of God alone, he may not cause the growth that we want. Worse yet, if we completely abandon our will to God's, we worry that we may end up as the proverbial missionary to a pygmy tribe in deepest Africa!

I remember very clearly how I had to deal with this fear when I left my first ministry position as an associate pastor, because I knew beyond all doubt that God was calling me into the role of senior pastor. I had certain expectations and ideas regarding my first senior pastor position. I knew what it would look like and what would best suit me. I was looking for a nice, suburban church with between 200 and 400 members, an experienced staff, and a decent facility.

At the same time I was well aware that my district executive minister was very passionate about church planting and that once he got word of my resignation, he would suggest I plant a church. Church planting was the very last thing I was interested in doing. As a church planter, I knew there would be no nice facility, no office, no staff, no budget to speak of, and none of the other accoutrements I desperately needed to feel good about myself. *What if my district executive wanted me to be a*

113

church planter? Where might he want me to go? I dreaded the possibility of being sent to some forgotten piece of southern California desert with the task of starting a church for windmill operators or some other obscure and difficult assignment.

My fear of an unknown future was greatly disconcerting and created within me much anxiety. It just seemed so much safer and easier to follow my own predetermined course into the preferred future I had planned for myself. It was during this period that I first faced the battle between my personal plan and the sovereign plan of God for me.

Much to my chagrin, I was encouraged to consider taking on the challenge of planting a church in one of the most undesirable areas of southern California. It was not something I aspired to, but it was one of those times when deep within my soul I sensed this was a direction God was charting for me.

Ultimately I did accept the call to church planting that God made clear he was issuing to me. It was a call I accepted with fear and not a little disappointment. However, it was the very best experience I could have possibly had at that point in my life and ministry. Sometimes the most painful experiences are the most fruitful. I didn't say enjoyable or fun but fruitful. We often learn the most through pain rather than pleasure. I learned more about myself and my abilities during that assignment than I ever would have had I followed my own plan. It was an opportunity that laid the foundation for virtually everything that has taken place in my ministry life since. God knew what he was doing. My future was unknown to me, but God knew it perfectly before I was even born. My fear of the unknown almost prevented me from undertaking one of the best experiences of my entire life.

114

Fear of Loss

Another fear that can keep us from engaging in reckless trust is the fear that to do so may very well cause us to miss out on some great opportunity.

We're afraid that if we entrust everything to God and resist the temptation to give direction to our own ministry career, we may be passed over for important assignments or we will languish in some pastoral purgatory that will prevent us from realizing our dreams and goals in ministry. I mean, if we aren't keeping ourselves in the denominational limelight, how are our superiors ever going to be made aware of our considerable talents and abilities?

It is our fear of losing out and getting stuck in some invisible ministry post that often keeps us from recklessly entrusting our life to God. We have this warped perspective that we can somehow do a better job of advancing ourselves, taking full advantage of our gifts, than can the God who called and gifted us.

It is when we are forced to do battle with the fear of missing out on something exciting that we need to reflect on the truth of Psalm 84, where the psalmist says:

> A single day in your courts
>   is better than a thousand anywhere else!
> I would rather be a gatekeeper in the house of my God
>   than live the good life in the home of the wicked. . . .
> No good thing will the LORD withhold
>   from those who do what is right.
> O LORD Almighty,
>   happy are those who trust in you.

> Psalm 84:10–12

115

Do we truly believe that? Can we honestly say that it would be better to spend one day in the place of God's choosing than a thousand days in the place and position of our own creation? Have we gotten to the place in our life journey where we would be content to serve in the most humble, invisible role in God's kingdom rather than in some lofty, highly visible ministry post if that is what God has deemed best for us? Before we will ever be able to recklessly entrust our life and ministry to God, we will need to overcome our fear of loss.

Fear of Unrealized Dreams

We all have dreams. I am convinced that for many spiritual leaders they are dreams that have been planted by God. Many of us, however, forget our dreams are from God and we begin to hold on to them too tightly for fear that they may not be realized. We are afraid that if we release our dreams completely to God, we may not see them become reality, so we attempt to bring them to fruition through our own ingenuity and effort.

In Psalm 37 David wants us to understand that the best path to realizing the desires of our heart is to let go of them and recklessly trust God. David reminds us:

> Trust in the LORD and do good.
>   Then you will live safely in the land and prosper.
> Take delight in the LORD,
>   and he will give you your heart's desires.
> Commit *everything* you do to the LORD.
>   Trust him, and he will help you. . . .
> Don't be impatient for the LORD to act!
>   Travel steadily along his path.
> He will honor you, giving you the land.

Psalm 37:3–5, 34

It is only when we are able to hold our dreams and desires loosely enough to give them back to God, from whom they came, that we have the greatest potential of realizing them. Before we are able to recklessly trust God with our hopes and dreams for ministry, we will need to overcome our fear and entrust our dreams to God.

Fear of Failure

One final fear that often stifles our reckless trust is the fear of failure. For many high-octane leaders there is the fear that letting go of everything to trust God is synonymous with failure. We think that trusting God means we do nothing and just wait for everything to come to us. And we know what happens when we do nothing—we fail! So instead we are determined to take control of our destiny and create our success through our own diligent effort, and we fail to understand that trusting is not synonymous with doing nothing and the failure that usually results from such an approach.

Trusting God does not mean that we do nothing. We still work hard and pursue excellence in all we do. But in all of the strategizing, planning, working, and pursuing we are always cognizant of the reality that God alone is in sovereign control of the outcome. Overcoming our fear of failure to recklessly trust God means that we must begin to understand that we may be the ones who plant and water, but it is God who brings the growth. We work hard and with excellence, but we release the outcome to God.

We need to realize that some of the hardest work we will ever do is trusting God to do for us what we cannot do for ourselves. We shouldn't allow a fear of failure to prevent us from the reckless trust necessary for true

117

ministry success. It is only when we are recklessly trusting God that we cannot fail regardless of what our efforts produce.

Taking the Leap to Trust

Stepping off a two-hundred-foot cliff backward is not an easy or natural thing to do. In August of 2000, perched high above the city of Colorado Springs, that truth was reality for me as I prepared to rappel down just such a cliff as part of a team-building exercise. Though it was not my first rappelling experience, it was just as nerve-racking as the first time I participated in this extreme activity.

Every summer I lead a group of emerging church leaders on a weeklong wilderness experience that is a part of our Leadership Central Program.[3] The very first adventure in which we participate is rappelling. Though it is one of the most challenging and frightening adventures we engage in, we schedule it for day one because it is the best way to establish a rapport of trust among the team members.

If you have never rappelled before, it will be difficult for you to understand the emotions and thoughts that clutter the mind of someone who is waiting to step off the cliff. The first time I rappelled, I stood at the top of the sheer wall frantically wondering, *What if the rope breaks? Is my guide truly competent? How many times has he done this before? What happens if the carabiners connecting me to the rope fail to lock? Am I capable of executing the technique necessary for a controlled rappel, or will I mess up and make a quick trip to the bottom? Maybe I will be that one person in ten thousand that has an accident. Is my insurance up to date?* As my mind reeled with these and countless other ominous worries, my hands began to sweat profusely, my legs were weak and shaking, and my stomach developed a knot as my body was physiologically preparing me for this stressful experience.

So what exactly is it that makes rappelling such a stressful and frightening experience? Even after watching fifteen other people successfully rappel down the cliff, why would I be so worried and concerned about my safety? The critical factor that makes rappelling so difficult is *trust*. It requires an almost reckless trust. We must place our absolute trust in people and objects outside of ourselves, over which we have no control. We've got to trust the guide who is belaying us, and we must place our absolute trust in the equipment we are using—rope, carabiners, helmet, gloves, and boots.

In the final analysis the reason that rappelling is so frightening is because we are willingly placing ourselves in a situation over which we do not have complete control. Our successful execution of the proper technique is just one of many elements that must work together if the rappel is to be completed safely. We can do everything by the book, we can take every safety precaution and utilize the very best equipment, but that does not guarantee that we will achieve the desired objective. If just one of numerous elements breaks down, it spells disaster—equipment failure, staff incompetence, or personal carelessness can all create serious problems when you are rappelling. That's what makes rappelling an extreme sport—there are never any guarantees as to the outcome.

As a result of this uncertainty, every year there are members of our team who refuse to participate in the rappel. For whatever reasons, often reasons of which they themselves are not fully aware, some people cannot and will not place themselves in such a vulnerable position. Some people are not able to release control of

119

their life to the care of a guide or ropes and carabiners. For individuals of a more controlling nature, it is not easy to let go and trust that someone or something other than themselves will do what is best for them.

But for those who are able to muster the trust necessary to step off that cliff backward into midair, their life will never again be the same. Those willing to exercise such trust live life in a new way and at a new place, a place that those unable to live in reckless trust will experience only vicariously through the stories of others.

So what does this mean for us as leaders? For spiritual pilgrims who struggle to find success and significance through events over which we ultimately have no control, what does it mean to recklessly trust God? How can a church pastor, who desperately wants to see the church grow and its ministry expand, recklessly entrust it all to God?

We must learn to jump! In the words of author Brennan Manning, we must be willing to "Search [our] heart for the Isaac in [our] life—name it and then place it on the altar as an offering to the Lord—and we will know the meaning of Abrahamic trust."[4]

For some of us our Isaac is the deep desire for significant church growth and success in ministry. For others it is our own sense of personal security and safety that must be ruthlessly thrown on the altar. Recklessly trusting God means that the "Isaac" in our life, which prevents us from taking the leap of trust that allows God to truly be God in our life and work, needs to be jettisoned. It means that we must identify what we most desperately desire in our life, those things that are the objects of our greatest affection, and then let them go so that we can recklessly trust God to do what is best for us. Without this leap of trust we will never be able to experience the serenity that will restore the joy and delight to our life and ministry.

120

In the next chapter we will see that though our trust must be reckless, it is not without reason. As we will see, there is plenty to stimulate such reckless trust.

Suggestions for Self-Reflection

1. What is it that makes it most difficult for you to recklessly trust God with your future as well as every other aspect of your life and ministry? Be as specific as you are able.
2. Why do we often tend to believe (at some level) that we could actually create a more desirable future for our life and ministry than God can?
3. Review the fears given in this chapter that may prevent you from recklessly trusting God. Which of these fears do you struggle with the most? Why? Which fear do you struggle with the least and why?
4. Where do you think these fears come from?
5. Read Deuteronomy 1:29–33. In what ways can you identify with the children of Israel and their failure, in spite of all they had seen God do, to recklessly trust him for the Promised Land? How could your time in the "wilderness of distrust" be avoided?
6. Reflect on Psalm 84:10–12. What might God want to say to you through these verses?

SIX

Our Stimulus to Trust

The Sovereignty of God

The ability to trust God completely with our life, as well as the life of our church, cannot be manufactured in an experiential and spiritual vacuum through the exercise of nothing more than willpower. To exercise the reckless trust I have been advocating is not human. It violates every instinct and impulse that we have as human beings. There must be something that stimulates us to exercise this type of radical trust in a person whom we cannot see.

To recklessly trust God with every aspect of our life and ministry, particularly in the absence of any tangible inducements, demands that we receive help from some outside source. There must be a reason—some stimulus that can adequately motivate us to act contrary to our natural instincts.

During the course of teaching my son Sammy to swim, there came a point when he could progress no further in the acquisition of this new skill without exercising trust. In the early stages of that learning process

Sammy immensely enjoyed floating around the pool, buoyed by his water wings and Mickey Mouse life jacket. He was happy jumping in the pool and thrashing about with his friends because he had confidence that his water wings and life jacket would keep him afloat. The challenge for Sammy came when he outgrew his Mickey Mouse life jacket and the water wings would no longer fit around his rapidly growing arms. There's just something unnatural about a nine- or ten-year-old still floating around in the shallow end of the pool with flotation devices strapped to his body.

The summer that Sammy reluctantly jettisoned his water wings was an extremely challenging time for him—and me. I wanted to see Sammy experience the joy and freedom of exploring the entire pool under his own propulsion. I knew that such a milestone would produce for him increased self-confidence and personal growth. It would be a real personal victory. But Sammy was not quite as interested as I was in developing self-confidence and could have cared less about personal growth—he just wanted to swim.

Trying to convince my son that he could trust me as he was learning how to float and then swim without artificial aid required every bit as much influence and motivation as trying to change the constitution of our 130-year-old Baptist church. Talk about a tough sell! Every time I thought I had him convinced that it was okay for me to let go of him and that I was able to instantly assist him if he needed help, he would scream hysterically "No! Dad, don't let go!"

But over the course of several weeks, working with him several days each week, Sammy began to exercise more and more trust in my ability to help him should anything go wrong during an attempt at soloing. Whenever he got frightened and felt that he was sinking, I would just reach out and effortlessly lift him back to the

123

surface. Eventually Sammy learned that I could be trusted completely. Through experience he learned that his dad would not let him drown. Once he learned to trust me, Sammy learned to swim on his own that summer. It was a much-needed lesson in trust—one that we both needed.

For Sammy to let go and trust his father in the swimming pool required some outside stimulus. He needed to see and experience, not just once but on repeated occasions, that I could be trusted, that I was not going to let him sink to the bottom of the pool and just go about my business as if nothing had happened. Every time he experienced my ability to rescue him before he sank, his ability to trust me grew incrementally. Ultimately Sammy began to trust me without even thinking about it. Trusting me in the pool just became a natural response. He had learned from experience that I was trustworthy.

Learning to Trust

Like Sammy we all need to learn the lesson that our Father can be trusted completely. Unfortunately, learning to exercise reckless trust in our heavenly Father requires repeated exposure to those messy situations and events that evoke the need for trust. As Brennan Manning reminds us, "Salvation-history indicates that without exception trust must be purified in the crucible of trial."[1] Learning to trust God in this way is not something that takes place once for all time. It is an ability that grows stronger over time as we are repeatedly exposed to God's trustworthiness. As we begin to learn that God is in control of not only our own personal world but all of creation as well, we will gain a greater capacity to trust. But regardless of how many times God has proven he can be trusted, we will still be required to take that uncomfortable leap at what seems to be the most inconvenient and frightening of times. There will undoubtedly be those times when we feel like we're beginning to sink to the bottom of the pool and we frantically begin to wonder if our heavenly Dad will come through for us this time.

It is during those times that our understanding of the sovereignty of God has got to be much more than a concise statement in the *Evangelical Dictionary of Theology* that we can recite from memory. Truly understanding the sovereignty of God cannot be gained by taking Systematic Theology 101 alone. Though a conceptual understanding of God's sovereignty might be the place to begin, intellectual knowledge by itself will not enable us to place our "Isaacs" on the altar in reckless Abrahamic trust.

Understanding the sovereignty of God in a way that will stimulate us to recklessly trust God on a consistent basis will require that we allow ourselves to get bloodied and battered by the circumstances of life. Gaining the understanding that I am advocating is, indeed, a very painful and earthy process.

Just a couple of hours before writing this chapter at my local Barnes and Noble bookstore, I stopped at the hospital to see the father of one of our church's support staff. Tom, our staff member's father, is a godly man and a committed pastor. He has served God faithfully and energetically for many years. Recently he received a call to leave his rural church for a new ministry in the Minneapolis area, which he accepted. His first day in the pulpit at the new church was to be the first Sunday in January.

As Tom and his wife were preparing to move to their new home and begin their new ministry, he had a massive aortic aneurysm—his aorta ruptured from the heart

125

all the way into his abdomen. It was a truly lethal event that should have ended his life but for a sovereign intervention by God.

Tom was alone cleaning up their home and making plans to travel to meet his wife, who was already at their new home in Minneapolis. During the day as he painted and cleaned, Tom experienced discomfort in his stomach area but, as most men are wont to do, he shrugged it off as just being tired and overworked. When he was ready to leave and join his wife, he called his secretary to see if she was still interested in a television that they had talked about previously—did she want to come and take a look at it? he asked.

Though she hadn't planned on it, she decided on the spur of the moment to drive over and take a look. It was to be a five-minute visit to see a TV set. Moments after she arrived, Tom's aorta burst. Because the secretary was there at that precise moment, she was able to make the call that saved his life.

A coincidence? A lucky break? Not on your life. It was the sovereign act of God. After the surgery that saved his life, his family asked the ICU nurse how long it takes for people to recover from the type of surgery Tom underwent. Her response? "I don't know," the nurse said. "Most of the people who are brought in here with this type of aneurysm are already dead when they get here."

Though this episode has been a painful and messy experience for Tom and his family, they have learned some things about the sovereignty of God that they could have learned in no other way. Tom has learned that his new church will make it just fine without his preaching during this absence, because God is in sovereign control of his church. The growth and health of the church he serves is ultimately God's responsibility, not Tom's. Once he gets out of the hospital, he will be able to approach his ministry with a new measure of calm and confidence, having learned through experience that God is in control.

What Is God's Sovereignty?

The fourth edition of the *American Heritage Dictionary* defines sovereignty as ". . . the exercise of supreme authority or rule; the exercise of unmitigated power and authority."

According to well-known evangelical theologian Millard Erickson, God's sovereignty means that he has complete independence, as well as absolute and ultimate authority and power in the exercise of his care and direction over all his creation. Because he is the sovereign of the cosmos, God is the supreme ruler and lawgiver regarding all that pertains to his creation.[2] There is nothing that happens in all of his creation that he did not either cause, allow, endorse, or decree.

However, this does not mean, as many have wrongly concluded, that God is somehow the creator or cause of sin and evil. Rather, in his sovereignty God is able to utilize even the sinful choices of his creatures to bring about his ultimate purposes for them and his kingdom. Though God is in no way to be associated with the source of sin or evil, he omnipotently and sovereignly redirects the sinful acts of people and even of Satan in such a way that they become the very means of doing good.[3] In the words of Millard Erickson, God's sovereignty means that ". . . our omnipotent God is able to allow evil men to do their very worst, and still he accomplishes his purposes."[4] This is what Paul means when he states in Romans 8:28, "And we know that God causes *everything* to work together for the good of those who love God and are called according to his purpose for them."

In other words, God is in complete and total control of every aspect of all that he has created. Believe it or not, that includes our life and the life of the church that we serve as well! God did not engage in the creative act and then abandon his creation, leaving it to make its own chaotic and spasmodic way through the eons. God created everything with intention and for a specific purpose and consequently he provides direction and guidance to ensure that his purposes are realized in every detail. Because God is the supreme ruler and lawgiver, the creation cannot alter in any way what God has determined to do.

The apostle Paul knew well the supremacy and sovereignty of God and completely embraced it. In Colossians 1:15–17 Paul affirms:

> Christ is the visible image of the invisible God. He existed before God made anything at all and is supreme over *all* creation. Christ is the one through whom God created everything in heaven and earth. He made the things we can see and the things we can't see—kings, kingdoms, rulers, and authorities. *Everything* has been created through him and *for* him. He existed before everything else began, and *he holds all creation together.*

A little closer to home, when we apply God's sovereignty to each of us individual creatures, it means, "[We] can make many plans, *but the LORD's purpose will prevail*" (Prov. 19:21). Because God is sovereign over our life, it means that our "Human plans, no matter how wise or well advised, *cannot stand against the LORD*" (Prov. 21:30).

As a result of this reality, James warns us against the arrogance of attempting to live an autonomous life apart from the recognition of God's sovereignty when he says:

128

Look here, you people who say, "Today or tomorrow we are going to a certain town and will stay there a year. We will do business there and make a profit." How do you know what will happen tomorrow? For your life is like the morning fog—it's here a little while, then it's gone. What you ought to say is, "If the Lord wants us to, we will live and do this or that." Otherwise you will be boasting about your own plans, and all such boasting is evil.

James 4:13–16

But honestly, isn't this exactly what we often attempt to do in our efforts at producing church growth and ministry expansion? We determine the best course of action for the church and then decide what programs or methodologies we will employ to produce the desired result—often with little or no attention given to God's sovereignty in the matter. We forget that little part about, "If the Lord wants us to."

As a result, when our plans don't materialize exactly as we had planned or our efforts are thwarted by opposition or unexpected obstacles, rather than sensing that these might actually be the sovereign actions of God bringing about the modification or redirection of our plans, we respond to these unexpected changes with anger, frustration, depression, and a host of other responses that clearly demonstrate we have forgotten about the sovereignty of God in our pursuit of church growth and ministry success.

It is absolutely vital that we learn to factor in the sovereignty of God in all of our ministry efforts. How much time have we devoted to seeking his direction for our church—I mean really? Are we holding our plans loosely enough so that when circumstances change and our plans must be modified, or aborted altogether, we are readily able to let go of them and change course, sensing that God is sovereignly at work moving us in *his* direction?

Do we recognize that God works through other people as well as us? Just because we are the "professional" or the paid staff person, it does not necessarily mean that our plans are always the right plans. If God could speak to Balaam through a donkey, I think it's safe to assume he can speak to us and sovereignly direct his church through the people he has placed around us—whether they are believers or not.

You see, the painful reality is that whenever we feel threatened by the thought of someone tinkering with *our* plans, whenever we become paranoid that people are clandestinely attempting to modify *our* plans in an effort to do things differently, it is clear that we are holding on to our plans much too tightly. When this begins to happen, it is because our ministry is more about us and the realization of our success than it is about God and realizing his purposes and plans. Understanding God's sovereignty means that we are able to "go with the flow" a little more, knowing with confidence that God is in control of his church.

Seeing the Sovereignty of God in Action

Throughout biblical history God has demonstrated his sovereignty to many people and leaders. And one of the ways we can be stimulated to recklessly trust God, in addition to the experiences of our own life, is to read the stories and reflect on the experiences that God used to teach these people that he could be recklessly trusted. We see how God accomplished his purposes in spite of unplanned tragedies, changed plans, outright opposition, and even the evil intentions of those opposed to the leader.

130

In fact throughout the Scriptures we can see examples of how God sovereignly orchestrated the lives of men and women, without any help from the individuals themselves, to accomplish the most extraordinary assignments. God seems to delight in using those people who were not plotting and planning to get themselves ahead but who were somewhat obscure and, from a human perspective, very unlikely candidates for some strategic assignments.

Most of the biblical characters God used to accomplish his purposes and advance his kingdom plan did so as they were led by God down paths that they would have never dreamed of following on their own. With God it seems that the best way to get from point A to point B is *not* a straight line. Most often God charts a course for his servants that does not make good human sense at first glance and, in fact, often seems contrary to what we would consider the most prudent and sensible method for moving ahead in ministry. Countless times God interjected other people in the paths of these biblical examples, sovereignly thwarting their plans and efforts, all so that they could be redirected to the course that God had planned for them. Consider, for example, Noah, Job, Jonah, Nehemiah, and Gideon.

Though many of these great leaders responded to the interruptions God made in their lives with anger, frustration, confusion, and fear, we have the opportunity to learn from their experiences so that we do not repeat the negative responses.

We can see God's sovereignty in the life of Abraham. Abraham was a man God used to begin the family tree of Jesus the Messiah. God had a plan for Abraham's life that did not always unfold in the way and time that most people would consider strategic or reasonable.

In Genesis 12:1–3 God reveals his amazing plan for Abraham's future when he tells him:

Leave your country, your relatives, and your father's house, and go to the land that *I will show you. I will cause* you to become the father of a great nation. *I will bless you and make you famous, and I will make you a bless-ing* to others. *I will bless* those who bless you and curse those who curse you. All the families of the earth will be blessed through you.

This was a plan that God was going to orchestrate and flesh out for Abraham's life. Notice the repetition in these verses of "I will" as it pertains to who will bring these things about in Abraham's life. Abraham would not be required to plan out his life and strategize ways to advance himself and the plan. Abraham's responsi-bility was to be attentive to God's working in the cir-cumstances of his life and then follow his leading, and his initial response to this overwhelming and open-ended plan was obedience: "Abraham departed as the Lord had instructed him" (v. 4).

As we know from the story of Abraham's life, God did not immediately explain the entire plan. He didn't cause it to happen quickly or in what we might consider a direct and reasonable manner. Though the plan for Abraham's life was clear, the realization of the plan would require a lifetime of recklessly trusting God even when the directions God gave him didn't make any human sense at all.

I'm sure that Abraham wondered why God was prom-ising him a land that was already occupied by hostile people; why not establish this great new nation in unin-habited territory? That would make more sense. Once he got to the land God had promised him, Abraham was faced with a serious famine that forced him to flee to the land of Egypt. That didn't make sense!

God revealed that this great nation would begin with a child that Abraham's wife, Sarah, would bear, in spite

132

of the fact that she and Abraham were both beyond childbearing years. This was one of those occasions when Abraham's faith faltered and he and Sarah devised their own plan in an effort to help God out. Surely God couldn't have meant that he and Sarah would conceive the child by natural means. That would be impossible! So, rather than trusting God to produce the child of promise, they decided to navigate their own course in this matter and it resulted in a mess that is still with us to this day.

Over and over again in the life of Abraham we see that when he trusted God, promises were fulfilled in amazing ways. But whenever Abraham took matters into his own hands, he actually experienced frustration and failure.

We see much the same thing in the life of Joseph. God had a plan for Joseph's life, a plan that was to play a pivotal role in God's overall kingdom purposes. But again, just as with God's plan for Abraham, his plan for Joseph's life did not unfold in a way that Joseph would have charted for himself.

He was sold into slavery by his brothers and carted off to Egypt. During his early years in Egypt, he was falsely imprisoned and treated unfairly by the very people he had helped. Ultimately he was promoted to a position of great authority and power, which God used to preserve the lineage of the Messiah and keep his kingdom plan on course.

Throughout his life Joseph had to learn to trust God with his future even when all of the circumstances of the present seemed to be reeling out of control and making no sense whatsoever. But through it all Joseph was able to realize that God had been sovereignly at work in his life, bringing about his perfect plan for him. He acknowledged to his brothers: "As far as I am concerned, God turned into good what you meant for evil. *He brought me* to this high position I have today *so I could save the lives of many people"* (Gen. 50:20).

Once again we see God accomplishing amazing things and advancing his purposes through the life of a leader by means and methods that would have never been considered or planned by the leader himself.

Success for Joseph required trusting God even when life didn't make sense. Joseph had to believe that God knew what he was doing and that he would work all of the convoluted, seemingly disconnected events of his life into a cohesive whole.

In the life of Moses we observe a similar pattern. Again we see that God's method for getting people from point A to point B is not always a direct course. God charted a unique course for Moses—a course that was sovereignly plotted so that Moses could make unique contributions to the advancement of God's overall kingdom plan.

Moses had a desire to see his people liberated from their slavery in Egypt. When he attempted to achieve the plan in his own way, it led to a significant failure and a prolonged period of education and preparation in the desert of Midian. When the time was right, however, God knew where to find Moses and was able to communicate his plans for him in a convincing way. Moses' responsibility was to trust that God knew what he was doing and respond in faith. Throughout his life Moses learned how to trust God and walk in faith as his role in God's plan was progressively revealed over time.

Esther is another biblical figure whom God used in amazing ways that she could have never anticipated or planned. As a young woman Esther was taken as a slave to Persia's capital city of Susa. While she was there, a plot to exterminate the Jews was hatched by Haman, a nobleman who was scheming to advance himself and promote his own career.

134

Obviously the extermination of the Jews who were in captivity would strike a devastating blow to God's redemptive plan. But God had sovereignly orchestrated events in the life of Esther so that she would be in the right place at the right time to contribute to God's kingdom plan—even if it hadn't made sense up until this point.

When Esther's uncle, Mordecai, uncovered the plot to exterminate the Jews, he made the plot known to Esther, who had been elevated by this time to the position of queen. As she processed the information given to her by Mordecai and considered what action, if any, she should take, Mordecai made a profound statement:

> Don't think for a moment that you will escape there in the palace when all other Jews are killed. If you keep quiet at a time like this, deliverance for the Jews *will arise from some other place,* but you and your relatives will die. What's more, *who can say but that you have been elevated to the palace for just such a time as this?*
>
> Esther 4:13–14

What an intriguing and revealing statement Mordecai made here! He implied that God had placed Esther in a position to make a unique contribution to his kingdom plan. Mordecai's statement revealed that God was not so much concerned with orchestrating the events of Esther's life so that she would feel fulfilled and successful, but rather so that she could participate in what God was already in the process of doing. God was intent on saving his people; that was his plan. In fact Mordecai clearly stated that should Esther opt not to participate in God's rescue and salvation of the Jews by intervening with the king, God's plan would not be thwarted. God would still save the Jews by another means. The amazing thing was that God had sovereignly positioned

Esther to participate with him in what he was going to do. This was not something that Esther could have ever planned for her life. Regardless of how diligently or wisely she may have planned a potential "career path," Esther could have never even come close to planning a future that would rival what God had in mind for her.

In the lives of Abraham, Joseph, Moses, and Esther, as well as countless other biblical figures too numerous to mention here, God demonstrates that he is able to orchestrate the events of our life in such a way as to position us to participate in his kingdom plan in amazing ways!

Knowing Our Part and God's Part

Our part in the drama is to recklessly trust God with our life and constantly remain sensitive to his direction through the circumstances and opportunities he presents.

Rather than attempting to plot out our life and ministry as a way of realizing personal success, our job is to maintain a close relationship with God. Our central concern in life and ministry should be attentiveness to the working of God's Spirit, so that we are able to discern when he is opening or closing doors for us that will enable us to participate with him in new and more significant ways.

The Bible constantly reminds us that our life is about God's plan not ours—our life is about finding the right times and places to participate in what God is doing. He has a plan for us personally, as well as his divine, cosmic plan in which he desires to use us.

In each of the stories we just reviewed, we can see very clearly how God sovereignly works in the lives of people to direct them to the course he planned for them.

In each of these lives we see the truths of Scripture come to life and we can begin to trust that just as God was sovereignly at work in their lives, he is also at work in ours. We simply need to learn to sense his actions and follow his directions rather than resist them as we too often do.

Either we believe the Bible or we don't. Look at what the Bible has to say about our life and the reality that we are on a course charted by God himself. As David reflected on his life and the course God had charted for him, he writes:

> O Lord, you have examined my heart
>> and know everything about me.
> You know when I sit down or stand up.
>> You know my every thought when far away.
> You chart the path ahead of me
>> and tell me where to stop and rest.
> Every moment you know where I am. . . .
> You both precede and follow me. . . .
> Such knowledge is too wonderful for me,
>> too great for me to know!
>
> Psalm 139:1–6

Later in the same psalm David goes even further when he states:

> You saw me before I was born.
>> Every day of my life was recorded in your book.
> Every moment was laid out
>> before a single day had passed.
> How precious are your thoughts about me, O God!
>
> verses 16–17

I might not be a Hebrew scholar, but as I read these verses, it just seems to me that God has a plan for our

137

life! Every day of our life recorded? Every moment laid out before we had lived a single one? If we believe that is true, as we claim to, then what in the world are we worried about? Why do we burn ourselves out in frenzied activity and worry that some parishioner may keep us from achieving our purpose or prevent us from realizing God's plan for our life when the Bible clearly states that God has mapped out our life, beginning to end? There isn't a person alive who is going to prevent us from realizing all God has for us, and the lives of Abraham, Joseph, Moses, Esther, and countless others should stimulate us to recklessly trust God with our life and ministry as well.

As I mentioned in chapter 5, Paul confirms David's words in Psalm 139 when he writes: "For we are God's masterpiece. He has created us anew in Christ Jesus, *so that we can do the good things he planned for us long ago*" (Eph. 2:10). And Paul knew this truth experientially; he knew that God had charted a specific course for his life while he was still in his mother's womb, just as David wrote (see Galatians 1:15–17).

The challenge for us—and this is where the trust comes in—is that we can't see God's plan. We weren't born with a Rand McNally life map in our hand showing every twist and turn in our life. As a result we tend to believe our successful future depends on our own efforts. Sure, God works through our efforts, as we have seen, but he is in no way dependent on them or limited by them. Reviewing how God has worked in the lives of biblical characters may help to increase our ability to trust. At the same time, recognizing the ways that God has already been sovereignly at work in our own life can provide even greater stimulus to recklessly trust him in every area of our life in the future.

This is where our journal can become an invaluable tool in learning to trust God with our future. As we

138

review how God has led us to our present place, we quickly begin to see how God has sovereignly protected us and directed us through events over which we had no control. And if he did it in the past, we can trust that he will continue to do it in the future as well.

As I have reflected on my life and the life of my extended family, I can clearly see the sovereign hand of God at work in even some of the most tragic and painful events our family has experienced. God has been at work guiding me in the direction he planned for me since before I was born, and he has used events over which I had absolutely no control to profoundly impact the ultimate course of my life.

On a sunny Sunday morning in 1965 my father was on his way home from running a short errand, coming to pick the rest of us up for a family outing to our cousin's house. As my dad exited the freeway that morning, an exit he had taken thousands of times before, he ran the four-way stop sign at the top of the exit and plowed into a Volkswagen beetle driven by a woman named Anna, who was on her way to church that morning.

Anna, a Christian, was killed in that accident and my father was devastated. In the aftermath of that tragedy a young pastor and his wife, who had just moved into our neighborhood, read about the accident in the paper and realized that they lived only six houses away from our family. Bob and Ramona Griffin took the initiative to visit my parents, bringing a pie and offering to help in any way they could. Seeing that my parents were deeply troubled both emotionally and spiritually, they extended an invitation to attend the church at which Bob had just assumed the senior minister position.

Within a couple of weeks my parents did attend that church. Shortly after that first visit they heard the gospel of Christ clearly presented and together they walked down the center aisle of that little white church, committing their lives to Christ. From that day my parents have continually grown in their faith and Christian involvement. Bob and Ramona Griffin and their family became our family's closest friends. My father and mother served in that church in every position imaginable for nearly thirty years.

Today not only am I in full-time Christian ministry, but my younger brother, Mike, is also a pastor, and my youngest brother, John, and his entire family are committed followers of Christ. My sister, Candi, is also an active Christ follower.

The human reason I am in pastoral ministry is largely due to the life example of Bob Griffin. But the real reason is because that is a part of the course God charted for me before I was born. Did I freely choose to enter pastoral ministry? Yes, every step of the way I have freely chosen the path leading to full-time pastoral ministry. But the supernatural, sovereign reality is that God laid out every moment of my life before I had lived a single second. God used Bob Griffin in my life as a catalyst to accomplish his sovereign purpose for me.

In this and so many other details of my life I have seen the sovereign hand of God guiding, protecting, and motivating me. He has brought opportunities into my life and presented me with numerous choices—some that I have responded to positively, while there have been others that I have rejected completely. But in it all I am beginning to see that I am "God's masterpiece," created to do the good things that God planned for me to do from long ago.

So does that mean that as a pastor, I never worried about the direction of my life and the growth of our church? Did I ever work myself into a lather about low offerings, departing families, and members of the congregation who wrote me nasty ministry "fan mail"? It would be a lie to say that I never did. But I can report that as I began to focus more and more on the sovereignty of God that I have seen played out in the lives of biblical characters, human history, and the details of my own life, the unexpected twists and turns of this life have increasingly lost their stress-inducing, frustration-creating, depression-producing power over me.

I am beginning to look at my life, the life of the organization I serve, and my future destiny as a very small part of a much bigger picture, a picture that was painted and completed in every detail long ago, before I was born. More and more frequently, I am choosing to not obsess about my future and where I will be ten years from now, wondering whether or not I will be "successful," opting instead to keep my eyes and heart wide open to sense God's sovereign guidance moment by moment as the journey that is my life unfolds before me.

Understanding and experiencing the sovereignty of God has provided an amazing stimulus that has enabled me to recklessly trust God on a more consistent basis than at any previous time in my life. I am beginning to learn, much too slowly, that God *does* know what he is doing with and in my life, even during those times when I do not.

I am learning that if I seek God's will first, and remain spiritually sensitive, God will provide the direction, stimuli, clues, counsel, courage, and everything else I need to accomplish all he has planned for me to accomplish. Whether my books sell millions or merely hundreds. Whether I pastor a church of thousands or fifty. If I never speak at a national pastor's conference or if I have the privilege of speaking to presidents and world leaders. Whether I am blessed with financial abundance or am required to eke out my material existence. Wherever I am, whatever I have or have to do, I am learning that it is the place of God's design and where I am meant to be.

The more I grow in the experiential understanding of God's sovereignty, I find myself longing for the words of a popular praise song, "Lord, Reign in Me," to be the prayer and reality of my life.

> Over all the earth, you reign on high
> Every mountain stream, every sunset sky
> But my one request, Lord, my *only* aim
> Is that you reign in me again.
>
> Lord, reign in me, reign in your power
> Over all my dreams, in my darkest hour.
> You are the Lord of all I am
> So won't you reign in me again?
>
> Over every thought, over every word
> May my life reflect the beauty of my Lord,
> 'Cause you mean more to me than any earthly thing,
> So won't you reign in me again![5]

Let me reiterate, at the risk of being redundant, that my recognition of God's sovereignty does not mean that I use it as an excuse for sloppy ministry or second-best efforts. Embracing God's sovereignty in my life and ministry does not give me liberty to be lazy with the excuse of "letting God be God." Rather, I will always give my best effort, planning diligently and casting God-sized vision for the organizations that I am called and privileged to serve, because I know that wherever I am and whatever I am doing I am there and doing it because it is where God has me, and he requires the very best I have to give.

When we finally begin to understand the sovereignty of God in an experiential way, it will provide the stimulus that we need to recklessly trust God with our life and ministry. Similarly, as we will see in the next chapter, understanding that God exercises his sovereignty in the context

142

of an overwhelming, virtually indescribable love for us, will enable us to consistently experience an abiding serenity regardless of the circumstances and events of our life.

Suggestions for Self-Reflection

1. Why is recklessly placing our trust in a loving, all-knowing, all-powerful, sovereign God so difficult for us?
2. Review the definition of God's sovereignty on page 127. In light of the technical definition, what exactly does God's sovereignty mean to you in your life—what ramifications should the sovereignty of God have for the way you go about living and serving?
3. Take some time to reflect on Proverbs 19:21 and 21:30 and their implications for your life and ministry.
4. As you think about the sovereign actions of God in the lives of Abraham, Joseph, Moses, and Esther (pages 131–36), what can you learn about trusting God to do through you what you could never do on your own?
5. Meditate on Ephesians 2:10 and Galatians 1:15–17. What might God want to communicate to you through these biblical truths in light of where you are and what you are doing at the present time?
6. On a scale of 1 to 10, 10 being absolute reckless trust and 1 being an inability to trust God at all, where would you place yourself right now? Before you will be able to advance up this scale, what will need to happen in your life?

SEVEN

God's Loving Sovereignty

The Source of Our Serenity

Though an understanding of God's sovereignty may well be sufficient to stimulate us to recklessly trust him, God's sovereignty alone is not enough to provide us with an abiding sense of serenity that is able to transcend the events and circumstances of life. If we are to enjoy a measure of serenity in the living of our life and the pursuit of our ministry, we must be convinced that God always exercises his sovereignty in the context of an overwhelming, indescribably awesome love for us as his children.

The truth of the matter is that one can be a sovereign without being good. Numerous despots down through history have demonstrated that just because a person exercises unrivaled sovereignty, it does not necessarily follow that he or she will exercise sovereignty with benevolence. The likes of Jezebel, Nero, Attila the Hun, Adolf Hitler, Nicolae Ceausescu, and Slobodan Milosevic remind us that people who possess supreme power and authority are, more often than not, prone to the exploitation and destruction of those over whom they exercise their sovereignty. We as creatures do not have an abundance of good experiences with loving, benevolent sovereigns. Actually, the opposite seems to be truer.

As a result, it is often difficult for us to find much peace or serenity in thoughts of recklessly entrusting our life and ministry to God. What guarantee do we have that God will do what is best for us? How can we be sure that God won't just toy with us and mercilessly watch us writhe in agony as we confront the trials and tribulations of life? What guarantee do we have that God won't dangle a dream in front of us or plant within us a deep desire to find transcendent purpose by serving him in some arena about which we are passionate, but never allow us to fully connect with that passion or dream?

The guarantee that God gives us is his love. It is a guarantee written and sealed in the blood of his son, Jesus Christ. Clearly, a God who would willingly allow his son to experience a brutal, humiliating, and torturous death to accomplish what is best for us will most certainly go to whatever measures necessary to ensure that his good purposes for our life are realized. It is an experiential understanding of God's amazing love for us, and the realization that he always exercises his sovereignty in the context of that love, that will enable us to consistently experience a degree of serenity that transcends the events and circumstances of this life no matter how vexing they may become.

This means that when our church is not growing as fast or to the extent to which we think it should, we can still move ahead in our ministry unaffected and unworried. It means that when we don't get the position that we desperately wanted, we are still able to enjoy a measure of calm that transcends our circumstances. When the offering totals are going south and the attendance figures aren't far behind, when our latest outreach efforts

145

don't produce the results we had hoped for, and when we're facing criticism and complaints, even then we can remain unruffled and calm, knowing that God is in loving control of every aspect of our life and ministry.

Whether we are called to endure heart-hollowing betrayals, ugly church splits, staff mutinies, an elder board of late or never adopters, or a ministry that is relatively invisible on our denominational landscape, we can find a deep, abiding, consistent sense of inner serenity as we firmly grip the reality that God's sovereignty is always exercised in the context of his irrational, inexplicable, ravenous love for us. In fact the biblical reality is that every event with which we are confronted, each difficulty we must endure, and every emotion we experience will eventually work for our eternal good. Such is the sovereign love of our Father for each of his children.

Finding the Serenity We Seek

So what exactly is this serenity that I have been writing about since the beginning of this book? What precisely does it mean to find serenity in God's sovereignty?

To be serene is to be unaffected by disturbance. To experience serenity is to be calm and unruffled in the face of uncertainties and the inevitable trials and tribulations of life. Finding serenity in God's sovereignty means that no matter what situation we find ourselves in and regardless of the challenges we face, we are, for the most part, calm and unruffled. It means that we are able to remain unaffected by the disturbances and circumstances that life throws at us, regardless of what they may be.

During the war in Serbia, I saw a riveting picture in one of the newsmagazines that perfectly depicted the type of serenity I am attempting to describe. It was the picture of a young mother holding an infant. That young mother's face was smeared with dirt and grime and her clothes were filthy and torn. In the background was her home—at least what used to be her home—its walls peppered with bullet holes and its interior smoldering after a recent bombing raid. There was a tank rumbling in the background between the mother and the remains of her home. And in the midst of all the chaos and human anguish, that little baby slept and its face was the perfect picture of tranquillity, completely oblivious to all of the tragedy that was unfolding around it. That little baby had a face that said, "I am safe. All is well. I am in my mother's arms and she will take care of me no matter what happens."

That is truly what God desires for us. He wants us to rest in his sovereign care knowing that he has everything completely under control and that nothing will enter our lives unless he deems it is in our best interest eternally. It is the type of attitude expressed by Job when he finally reaches that place where he can say, "Though he slay me, yet will I trust him," knowing that God will ultimately do what is best for him even if that means allowing his premature, unjust death.

Many of the people that I have met in ministry are experiencing anything but this kind of serenity. Too many of us spiritual leaders and pastors live lives and lead ministries that are characterized by stress, worry, frenetic activity, and a level of emotional and spiritual chaos that is unhealthy both for us and for the people we lead. Much of this stress and anxiety is produced by our need to succeed and accomplish something of value. Or the stress is produced by our fear that the church leaders we serve with will grow weary of no growth or slow growth and begin making plans for a new pastor who will be better able to produce.

147

Many pastors are unable to relax and truly enjoy their ministry because they are afraid that if they do—if they ease up in their efforts for even one minute—everything they have worked so hard for and all that they are basing their personal value and worth on might crumble before them, rendering them a worthless failure—at least in their own eyes.

During my years as a church planter I don't believe I experienced a single moment of serenity as I have just described it. I cannot remember a single time when I was truly unruffled or unaffected by the challenges and difficult circumstances that seemed to constantly confront me as I attempted to establish that church.

I lived in the constant fear that each Sunday would be the Sunday that no one showed up. For most of my years as a church planter I felt as if I were holding that fledgling congregation together by the sheer power of my personality and, if I let down for even an hour, the whole thing might fall down around my ankles, declaring undeniably to all observers that I was an unmitigated failure and that I had no future in church ministry.

As a result, every sermon needed to be a "home run" to keep the people coming back. Every counseling session needed to produce a life-changing breakthrough. Each of our special events needed to exceed in quality and attendance the previous event we conducted. I felt that we needed to provide worship music that was second to none and offer a range of services that would meet the needs of the largest number of people possible. I needed to ensure that the giving remained strong and that we had the resources necessary to keep aggressively moving ahead. I was desperate to make sure we didn't lose momentum and that we didn't concede any of our hard-won progress.

I felt that it was vital to maintain absolute control over every aspect of our infant church if it was going to survive. Nothing could be left to chance. And so, understandably, whenever we were threatened by a low offering, a major defection, or a less-than-stellar Sunday morning service, I was absolutely devastated and overcome with feelings of gloom and impending disaster.

The only solution was to work harder and do everything possible to ensure that there would be no such setbacks in the future. At no time did I stop to reflect on the reality that God was in absolute control of that church plant. Sure, at some intellectual and theological level I suppose I knew that it was true, but it certainly wasn't a truth that had successfully escaped my intellect to positively affect the way I was living and conducting ministry. I lived and worked as if the whole church operation relied on me and me alone. How could anyone relax or enjoy a measure of serenity with that kind of unrealistic expectation constantly weighing on him?

In his book *Amazon.Com: Get Big Fast,* Robert Spector reveals how a desperate desire for success and an obsessive fear of failure has driven Amazon.Com creator, Jeff Bezos, to a place where friends and family fear for his emotional and physical health. Spector writes:

> An astute student of business, Bezos is keenly aware that the pioneers [of new business technologies] are not always the survivors. "I tell people around here to wake up petrified and afraid every morning," [Bezos] said. "I know we can lose it all. It's not a fear. It's a fact."[1]

It is that obsessive drive and fear of failure that has caused close friends to make comments such as:

> . . . [Jeff] is the most single-mindedly focused person I've ever met—to his detriment; it's all he cares about. He

149

lives, eats, breathes Amazon.com. It occupies virtually every waking moment. He is maniacally focused. I worry about his health. I worry about what he's going to be like when he's 50.[2]

Unfortunately, my inability to entrust my ministry and the future of the church to God resulted in a season of emotional and spiritual bankruptcy. Like Jeff Bezos, I had worked and worried myself to the point where I realized I could work or worry no more. I had nothing left in reserve. I had no resources from which I could draw to sustain myself in the face of one more ministry mess. There was nothing left for me to do but crash and burn. I was experiencing the depths of burnout.

How different my experience, or that of multimillionaire Jeff Bezos, has been from that of the apostle Paul! Not only was he facing difficulties and challenges in ministry and life that most of us couldn't even imagine, he was waiting for his head to be cut off in a foreign prison. His church plants were under constant attacks from within and without. His life had been in almost constant physical danger during most of his ministry. His motives were frequently impugned and his reputation regularly trashed. And yet, in spite of it all, Paul experienced an uncommon serenity and inner tranquillity that escapes many of us in ministry today.

In Philippians 4:11–13 Paul boldly and confidently asserts:

> Not that I was ever in need, for *I have learned* how to get along happily whether I have much or little. I know how to live on almost nothing or with everything. I have learned the secret of living *in every situation*, whether it is with a full stomach or empty, with plenty or little. For I can do everything with the help of Christ who gives me the strength I need.

150

The New Living Translation uses the phrase "get along happily," which is rendered "be content" in the New International and New American Standard versions. *Content* is a synonym for the word *serene*. What Paul is saying in these verses is that he has learned not to allow the circumstances of life to get him all riled up and stressed out. Whether his ministry efforts are going well or whether they are going poorly, regardless of his personal condition or material position, Paul says he has learned the secret of remaining calm and unruffled in every situation.

Paul had reached the place in his life and ministry where his internal state was no longer dictated by his degree of external success or achievement. The great apostle was using a different standard of measure, a standard that allowed him to experience a degree of serenity that transcended even the most difficult and trying of circumstances.

This is amazing to me. If the apostle Paul was not a "type A," compulsive, perfectionistic, "high I" type of leader, then there's never been one! You need only peruse Philippians 3 to see that Paul was an extremely driven, accomplishment-oriented individual. We're not talking about an introverted, touchy-feely, laid-back shrinking violet here. And yet, in spite of his natural personality traits and apparent competitiveness, Paul had learned to find inner calm and serenity even when his ministry plans were interrupted and his personal goals openly opposed.

Even as Paul was traveling the length and breadth of the Roman Empire, planting churches and establishing spiritual leaders to serve those churches, his efforts were constantly being curtailed by the false accusations of established religious leaders whose only concern was their own self-interest. But through it all, Paul still managed to maintain an eternal perspective and even pen an epistle of joy to other struggling leaders while he himself was in prison.

In the face of such an example I can't help but feel convicted and somewhat ashamed of my own feeble responses to the opposition my ministry efforts periodically face. Rather than focusing on the God who has called me and entrusting my ministry to him when opposition hits, my tendency has more often been to throw myself a little pity party and dwell on how unfairly I've been treated. From some of my pitiful responses and the inner chaos I allow those responses to create, you'd think I was being burned at the stake as a heretic.

What a difference there is between Paul's inner state and that of so many spiritual leaders in the church today! It seems that we have lost our focus on the sovereignty of God and on the reality that he exercises that sovereignty, controlled by his amazing love for us. Our frenzied inner state betrays the fact that we have forgotten that our purpose in life is to fulfill God's purposes and advance his kingdom, not to establish and build our own.

Is such an experience of serenity possible only for spiritual heavyweights such as the great apostle, or is there hope for you and me as well? Jesus said, "I am leaving you with a gift—peace of mind and heart. And the peace I give isn't like the peace the world gives. So don't be troubled or afraid" (John 14:27). Do we believe he was talking to us, or was this promised gift something intended for his first-century disciples only? If we believe, as we are prone to teach others, that this promise is for all followers of Christ, how can we go about learning, as Paul did, to make that kind of peace of mind and heart something we consistently experience in the context of our ministry?

The answer to that question, I have become increasingly convinced, lies not only in understanding and experiential embracing the sovereignty of God over our lives, but also in understanding beyond all reasonable doubt that God *always* exercises his sovereignty in the context of a love for us that defies human definition.

The Sovereign Lover of Our Soul

To consistently experience the type of serenity we have been discussing requires that we experience and relate to God as more than merely a benevolent dictator. We'll need to become convinced that he loves us beyond measure and will always and only do what is eternally best for us.

Not long ago I read about a king in the Middle East who receives respect and submission from his subjects not only because of his title and office. This king is a king like few others. He actually cares deeply about the people under his rule and he wants the very best for them. As a result, the people of the realm feel comfortable coming to him with their problems and troubles, having confidence that he will act on their behalf in a way that will be best for them. It is an uncommon love relationship that exists between this king and his people—a relationship that creates a sense of serenity among the people. When unforeseen troubles confront them and the tide of life unexpectedly turns against them, they are calm and unruffled because they know that their king will make everything right. Whether they need money to pay a debt, medical care, simple words of advice, or just about anything else, they know that their loving king will do what is best for them—because he truly loves them.

The truth is that we have a King who is more than just benevolent. Our King is utterly perfect in his love, wisdom, goodness, and concern for us. In fact he loves us so

153

much that there is not anything he will not do for us to accomplish what is eternally best for us as his children.

In Romans 8 Paul writes some of the most extraordinary, superlative words about the love of God ever to make their way from pen tip to paper.

> So you should not be like cowering, fearful slaves. You should behave instead like God's very own children, adopted into his family—calling him "Father, dear Father." For his Holy Spirit speaks to us deep in our hearts and tells us that we are God's children. And since we are his children, we share in his treasures—for everything God gives to his Son, Christ, is ours, too. But, if we are to share his glory, we must also share his suffering.
>
> Romans 8:15–17

Paul understood clearly that he was God's beloved child and that all God had done for and given to his Son Jesus was also a part of Paul's inheritance as a son of God. But he also recognized that this did not mean he would never have difficult times or struggles in his ministry. In the last verse of that passage Paul uses a conjunction of contrast to communicate that our status as children of God and objects of his love does not exclude the possibility of suffering and pain. In fact his point is that we should expect it in this life as we minister for him.

But even as he shared in the suffering of Christ, Paul was convinced that nothing in all of the world could ever keep God's plan and purpose for him from being ultimately realized.

Paul continues his reflection on God's sovereign love for us:

> What can we say about such wonderful things as these? If God is for us, who can ever be against us? Since God

did not spare even his own Son but gave him up for us all, won't God, who gave us Christ, also give us everything else? . . . Can anything ever separate us from Christ's love? Does it mean he no longer loves us if we have trouble or calamity, or are persecuted, or are hungry or cold or in danger or threatened with death? . . . No, despite all these things, overwhelming victory is ours through Christ, who loved us.

verses 31–32, 35, 37

And he continues his soliloquy on God's sovereign love:

And I am convinced that nothing can ever separate us from his love. Death can't, and life can't. The angels can't, and the demons can't. Our fears for today, our worries about tomorrow, and even the powers of hell can't keep God's love away. Whether we are high in the sky or in the deepest ocean, nothing in all creation will ever be able to separate us from the love of God that is revealed in Christ Jesus our Lord.

verses 38–39

Armed with this understanding of God's sovereign love, is it any wonder that Paul could write with absolute, unshakable confidence that he had learned the secret of being content or serene in any and all circumstances? The secret that Paul had learned, through experience as well as his understanding of the Scriptures, was that there was nothing in all of the cosmos that could prevent God's perfect plan for him from being fully realized.

Paul knew he didn't need to sweat the small stuff—and it was all small stuff to God! So when his ministry plans were opposed or he faced physical harm and difficult circumstances, he didn't allow them to crush him or make him feel like a failure. When the churches were not grow-

155

ing as rapidly as maybe he'd hoped or a new church plant didn't start as he'd planned, it wasn't a fatal blow to his ministry efforts. When the leaders he'd trained and released into ministry struggled and created unnecessary chaos in their churches, he didn't come unglued. Even when he was forced to spend his days in a dank, foul-smelling, cramped prison cell as a result of his ministry opponents' efforts to stifle his effective proclamation of the gospel, he could remain calm and unruffled. He knew beyond all doubt that even if he were imprisoned or killed, his work could not be snuffed out (see 2 Timothy 2:9).

Paul knew and fully embraced a spiritual reality that few of us today have embraced to the same degree—the God of the universe loved him, had called him, and was unequivocally for him, so that no one or nothing could ever be effectively against him.

I can't help but wonder how such an understanding would alter our perspective on ministry success in the twenty-first century if we were also able to embrace experientially that profound spiritual truth. If such a spiritual reality took root in our heart, I'm convinced that we would be able to experience the same degree of otherworldly serenity and peace that marked Paul's life.

A Love Higher than the Heavens

If the testimony of Paul is not enough to convince us of God's sovereign love for us and that nothing can prevent his plan and purpose for us from being realized, perhaps King David can succeed where Paul failed.

Though David experienced more than his fair share of difficulties and human tragedy, his understanding of God's unfathomable love for him spurred him to faithfulness until the very end of his life. In Psalm 103 David gives divinely inspired expression to his understanding of God's love for him. He writes, "For his unfailing love toward those who fear him is as great as the height of the heavens above the earth" (v. 11).

Now at first glance, without a careful reading and some deep reflection, the mind-boggling truth of this verse might possibly escape us—but it should not. When was the last time you actually stopped to ponder that statement? How long has it been since you allowed yourself to become lost in the wild, boundless, infinite cosmic expanse that is the heavens? It's not until we are reminded of just how high the heavens actually are above the earth that David's seemingly simple statement will begin to resonate in our hearts and minds.

Take just a moment to imagine with me that you were able to travel at the speed of light; that is 186,282 miles per second or 6,000,000,000,000 (that's six trillion) miles in one year. If you decided to explore just how high the heavens actually are above the earth by traveling to the edges of the vacuous expanse of space, your travelogue would go something like this:

- In just 4 minutes of traveling at 186,282 miles per second, you would reach the planet Mars.
- After 5 hours of travel at the speed of light, you would reach the planet Pluto.
- In 4.3 years you would arrive at the brightest, closest star in the galaxy, Centaurus.
- Continuing on at the speed of light, 186,282 miles per second, after 120,000 years of nonstop travel, you would reach the distant side of our own galaxy, the Milky Way.
- After 2 million years of continuous travel at the speed of light, you would finally reach Andromeda, the nearest large galaxy similar to our own, which is a part of a cluster of galaxies.

157

- In 22 million years you could reach the next nearest cluster of galaxies.
- After 8 billion earth years of nonstop travel at the speed of light, you could reach the farthest galaxy discovered to date, 3C123, which is believed by many astronomers to be moving away from the earth at one-third the speed of light!

Now what we need to begin grasping, if we ever hope to experience a measure of God's supernatural serenity, is the reality that as high as the heavens are above the earth, that's how great God's love for us is! It is a love that cannot be measured or contained by the limitless expanse of the cosmos. It is a love that cannot be given adequate expression by even the loftiest human language. Yet that is how much God loves us!

When we begin to finally grasp an understanding of God's sovereignty, and the reality that God always exercises that sovereignty in the context of his amazing, unutterable love for us, it will begin to generate within us a new measure of serenity and contentment regardless of the perceived success or failure of our ministry.

Understanding God's profound love for us, and the reality that he will always exercise his sovereignty in the context of that love, will lead to a redefinition of how we view personal and ministry success. It is to that redefinition of success we now turn in the next chapter.

Suggestions for Self-Reflection

1. What does God's love have to do with our finding true serenity in our life and ministry?
2. Take another look at the quotes about Amazon.com founder Jeff Bezos on pages 149–50. Can you relate

to him when it comes to the ministry of your local church? If so, in what ways?

3. Why do you think it is significant that the apostle Paul wrote that he had *learned* to be content in every circumstance? What does that say to you in your current circumstance?

4. What will have to happen in your life and ministry for Jesus' promise in John 14:27 to become a reality for you?

5. What is the difference between a theological understanding of God's love and the ability to personally experience it in all of its fullness? Do you consistently experience the love of God in your life?

6. If you struggle to believe, accept, and personally experience the truth that God loves you with a love that defies description, what do you think it is that prohibits that from happening in your life?

7. How do you think your life and ministry would change if you were able to unconditionally embrace the reality that God is in absolute, sovereign control of every aspect of your life and that he *always* exercises his sovereignty in the context of an indescribable love for you? Be as specific as you are able.

8. Why will experiencing God's love for you be a requirement before you will be able to consistently experience the serenity, contentment, and success that you seek?

9. What are those things in your life that currently create the greatest sense of anxiety and stress? How does the love of God speak to these issues?

10. If you are struggling in this area, what steps are you going to begin taking to deal with this vital spiritual issue? Write down a few action steps that you can begin taking immediately.

159

EIGHT

Redefining Ministry Success in Light of God's Loving Sovereignty

From Quantitative Result to Qualitative Experience

Growing up as I did in eastern Washington and the areas surrounding the mountains of north Idaho, I developed a love for the outdoors and hunting at a very early age.

As a twelve-year-old boy I remember the highlight of my year being the times that I would get to go deer hunting with my dad and uncles. It was always an exotic adventure for me that created so much anticipation and excitement that I could never sleep the night before we left for a deer hunt. I would wake up repeatedly during the middle of the night afraid that I had slept through the alarm or fearing that maybe Dad had decided to go without me this time. It was always a relief when I heard my father climbing the stairs to my room to roust me out of bed for the big hunt!

During my early years as a burgeoning outdoorsman, I felt that the success of a hunt was determined by whether or not we got what we were hunting for. As a twelve-year-old hunter my ultimate enjoyment of the hunt was directly related to what the hunt produced. *How could a deer hunt be deemed successful if you didn't come home with a deer?* I wondered.

Later, as I moved up to bird hunting, I initially measured my success in similar terms. If the limit for pheasants was three, then a successful hunt would produce three birds—anything less was a subpar hunt. For me as a young hunter, success was always measured quantitatively—how many of whatever it was we happened to be stalking did we put in the game bag or the larder?

Somewhere during my evolution as a hunter, and as a fly fisherman, the enjoyment I derived from the sport gradually became more about the quality of the experience than the quantitative result of the shooting or casting. Today, I am happy to report, I no longer measure the success of an outing by the number of birds I come home with or the size of the fish I catch. As a more mature hunter and fisherman my standard of measure for success has evolved over time to become almost exclusively qualitative as opposed to quantitative.

Now when I go on a hunt the success of the trip is measured in the quality of time spent afield and the quality of the relationships I enjoyed with my partners during the hunt. Today I get joy out of watching my dog, Ginger, cast back and forth across a golden field of picked corn until she suddenly stops in a rigid point, indicating that a bird has been found. One of the best hunts I have ever experienced was with my son Seth when he went on his first "real" bird hunt carrying his own shotgun. I can't even remember personally pulling the trigger on a bird that day. But seeing Seth's excitement and anticipation—the same excitement and antic-

161

ipation I experienced as a young boy all of those years ago—brought more joy and satisfaction to me than a whole truckload of birds.

As a result of my inner metamorphosis, my hunting has become infinitely more enjoyable and restorative. Today's hunts are no longer characterized by the stress of competition or the pressure to perform. I am no longer concerned with how my companions feel about the job my dog does or what they think of my shooting prowess. For me, my outdoor excursions have become more about the journey than they are about the destination, and, for that reason, they have become more fun than ever before.

A New Measure for Success

As I have confessed already, when I began in pastoral ministry, I was much more concerned, in fact almost exclusively concerned, with quantity as opposed to quality. When I began my ministry journey, it was not at all about the quality of the journey, but rather about reaching the destination as quickly and as impressively as possible. Every week saw me consumed with numbers: giving amounts, attendance figures, response numbers, visitor counts, and many other empirical standards of measure that gave irrefutable testimony to whether or not we had been successful for that week of ministry.

Let the numbers be down—even for one week—and I would be tumbling into a depressed state, scared to death that the end of my ministry was just around the corner and that any future advancement in ministry was in grave jeopardy. Frankly it was a miserable and destructive way to do ministry and live life.

During those years of obsessive and compulsive success seeking, I experienced periods of extreme stress and

162

the almost constant fear that we would lose some of our hard-won gains. This manic leadership style also created high levels of stress and performance anxiety in the lives of the leaders who led with me. Because virtually my entire identity and worth as a person was dependent on the success of our ministry endeavor, none of those leaders wanted to be the one who dropped the ball in such a way as to jeopardize our success. Though there was always a cordial spirit at our board meetings and times of equipping, in retrospect I sense that there was an awful lot of stress and anxiety just below the surface. They too were geared toward a performance mentality that I had unwittingly instilled and nurtured. Those faithful leaders who gave so sacrificially of themselves and their resources deserved better leadership than what I was able to provide them at that time in my life.

Fortunately, over the course of time, and as the result of a near emotional breakdown, God began the slow process of changing my warped perspective of success—particularly success as it relates to ministry. Over the course of the past ten years I have experienced an inner, spiritual metamorphosis that is something akin to the change that has taken place in the way I measure hunting success.

For me, success in ministry has become much more qualitative than it is quantitative. I no longer obsessively measure my accomplishments in terms of numbers and statistics as I did in my early years of ministry, seeing them as a direct reflection on my personal ability or worth as a person. For me success in ministry and life has begun to take on a much more spiritual and intangible meaning.

The reality is that it is entirely possible to manufacture phenomenal church growth and produce dramatic tangible indicators of success, while at the same time accomplishing nothing of any genuine eternal value. In

163

fact the realization of tangible signs of success in ministry can actually be the source of profound spiritual sickness and dysfunction both in a church and in the life of an individual leader.

Even as I write these words, I do so in absolute amazement that they are actually coming from my mind, and more shockingly, that I truly embrace the message that they attempt to convey. Not too many years ago I would have struggled with any propaganda such as this that attempted to convince me that genuine success in ministry cannot be empirically measured and is more qualitative in nature than it is quantitative. To me such notions were nothing more than excuses propagated by lazy or inept ministry practitioners in an attempt to assuage their feelings of failure at not being able to "produce" concrete results. I mean, if you can't produce tangible, measurable results, it only makes sense that you would want to lower the bar until you were finally able to declare yourself a success.

In other words, I thought such concepts of success were saying, "If you can't hit the mark, move the mark until you can hit it." Sadly, there are many spiritual leaders and ministry practitioners who feel the same way I did. However, in recent years some people are beginning to change their perspective as stressed-out and burned-out spiritual leaders are asking, "Is this all there is to success?"

The One-Minute Manager Searches for Success

In the business world too, leaders are beginning to think twice about the cost of success. Back in 1985 organizational management guru Ken Blanchard, coauthor of the phenomenally successful book *The One-Minute Manager,* began to question his own success. After he had sold millions of books, founded a prosperous consulting business, built a beautiful home and office in San Diego and a summer home in upstate New York, Ken began to feel that there had to be more to success. His growing sense of dissatisfaction led him on a journey to discover what genuine success really is and how it might be more accurately measured.

During the course of this journey to redefine success, Blanchard experienced a spiritual transformation as a result of contacts with Bill Hybels, pastor of Willow Creek Community Church, and Bob Buford, a successful Christian businessman based in Texas. In the wake of his spiritual rebirth, Ken Blanchard also began to see success in a new light, and his definition began an evolution of sorts. Describing this evolution he says:

> One of the things I started to realize is that if all you focus on is earthly success, you've got no chance of getting spiritual significance . . . if, however, you focus on spiritual significance, you've got a chance of earthly success. It really got to me to realize that the biggest addiction in the world today is the human ego . . . when you really start to look at why organizations get screwed up, it's because people at the top of the organization are pushing and shoving for wealth, achievement, recognition, power and status."[1]

Blanchard goes on to say, "When I started to really look at organizations in relation to my faith, it became so clear to me how confused people were about it. . . . They were all pushing and shoving for earthly success and not spiritual success."[2]

Unfortunately, these insights seem to be lost on many ministry leaders today. Because we work in the context of a spiritual organization, doing "ministry," it is easy

165

to delude ourselves into thinking that when *we* focus on tangible measures as a way to quantify and define our success, we are not succumbing to earthly definitions of success. But the reality is that when we focus primarily on empirical measurements for success, we are falling into a very dangerous trap—a trap that we must learn to avoid.

When Anticipated Success Doesn't Come

The earthly success trap that Blanchard speaks about is one that has seduced many committed spiritual leaders. One leader who learned firsthand the dangers of measuring success from an earthly perspective is well-respected pastor and author Kent Hughes.

After a successful stint as an associate pastor, Kent was given the assignment of starting a church in a rapidly growing area of southern California. Based on his previous ministry success, as well as his obvious and numerous gifts, his denominational officials knew that this would be a "gimme" for the denomination.

Kent and his wife, Barbara, also began this challenge having every reason to feel confident of success. After all, based on his track record, giftedness, a growing community, and substantial denominational support, how on earth could he fail? But things did not go as planned. In fact, by the second year of their church-planting effort, there were fewer people attending the church than the number they began with.

Forced to deal with the reality that the new church was not experiencing the much anticipated numerical growth, Kent began to struggle with feelings of failure and wondered whether God had actually called him to ministry in the first place. Maybe he had misunderstood

God's call. Worse yet, maybe God hadn't called him at all!

This professional crisis led to a full-blown search for the meaning of ministry success and failure. If your church isn't numerically growing, is it even possible to be considered successful in ministry? Conversely, when do you know if you've failed in ministry and it's time to call it quits? Though it was a personally painful and frightening process, it led to some liberating and life-giving discoveries that have characterized Kent's ministry ever since. Here, in his own words, is what Kent discovered about himself and his views of success in ministry:

> I had prided myself on my discriminating use of methods and principles. I thought God was certainly going to bless my ministry with great numerical growth because I was doing things "right."
>
> But I did not realize I had bought into the idea that success meant increased numbers. And since to me success in ministry meant growth in attendance, ultimate success was a big, growing church.
>
> Certainly, nothing is wrong with the wise use of church growth principles. Principles such as targeting a culture, keeping an eye toward visibility, and preaching biblically should be part of the intelligent orchestration of ministry.
>
> However, when the refrain they play to is numerical growth, when the persistent motif is numbers, then *pragmatism* becomes conductor. The audience inexorably becomes man rather than God, and subtle self-promotion becomes the driving force. Success in the ministry becomes the same as success in the world, and the servant of God evaluates his success like a businessman or an athlete or a politician.
>
> Given my thinking, the only conclusion I could derive was that I was failing. I knew what makes a church grow.

167

I had done my very best. I had little to show for it. Therefore I just didn't have what it takes. God had called me to a task without giving me the gifts to succeed, and I was justifiably bitter.[3]

Just as was the case with Ken Blanchard, Kent Hughes eventually developed a new view of ministry success.

I am convinced that until a person engages in the excruciatingly painful process of redefining success in light of God's sovereignty and other subtle spiritual realities, contentment and serenity in life and ministry will forever be an unrealized experience. Before we are ever able to experience the serenity and contentment that marked the life of the apostle Paul, we will be required to seek and embrace a new definition of success in ministry—a definition that has an eternal perspective and is in line with how God views success.

Seeing Success as God's Sovereign Gift

The task of redefining our understanding of success will not be an easy one. Over the course of a lifetime we have had drilled into us a cultural view of success that is not easy to shake.

Moreover, even if we are able to develop a new understanding of success from a biblical and eternal perspective, it will be a constant challenge for us to maintain that perspective and allow it to actually control and influence our motivations, decisions, and choices.

Everywhere we turn in our American culture the concept of success is synonymous with possessions, wealth, fame, and other tangible accoutrements. How could a person possibly consider himself successful if he has no home, owns no car, is flat broke financially, and is completely unknown in terms of his accomplishments?

This American obsession with material success begins for most of us at an early age. According to a *USA Today* poll, when asked to choose from a list of twenty-one different items and identify what they fantasize about the most and what would make them successful, 56 percent of teenage students polled said that success meant being rich. Another 43 percent said they fantasized the most about traveling the world, while 43 percent said success meant being famous.[4]

In fact every definition of *success* I found has as one of its first meanings the gaining of wealth or fame. Our cultural definitions of success gravitate around doing and the tangible results that give proof positive of the effectiveness of our doing. It is difficult, if not impossible, to find a definition of success that includes, or even references, in a minor way some aspect of being. You will not find any definitions of success that include such things as the ability to be content, the possession of integrity and character, or the ability to experience joy.

Success in America means producing results that can be seen by others. Success involves making a name for yourself and enjoying the good life. Is it any wonder then that we have adopted the same view of success when it comes to ministry and our personal lives as ministers or spiritual leaders? Though at some level we are no doubt uncomfortable with such reductionistic thinking, it is difficult to reject it entirely.

And so, even within the context of spiritual ministry, we have come to measure our success in exactly the same terms—sometimes subtly and subconsciously and sometimes not so subtly. Have we seen growth in our congregation or organization? Have we gained a degree of public recognition for what we have done? Do we enjoy some of the material benefits that seem to always accompany genuine success? If we are able to be painfully honest with ourselves, most of us would have to

169

admit that these worldly indicators of success are the same ones we use to measure success in our own life and the lives of others.

Sure, we may on occasion challenge the popular understanding of success and yearn for a more substantial and biblical definition, but inevitably we find ourselves quickly sucked back into mainstream thinking and find ourselves once again driven to achieve as our culture dictates.

It is hard to imagine Christian leaders paying $499 a person and flocking by the thousands to hear the advice and ideas of some pastor in Middle America who leads a church of 150. I mean, how could that pastor know anything about success?

In America, to qualify as a spiritual leader who is recognized as an authority on ministry, it is imperative that there be some tangible proofs that this person is worthy of an audience—popular books, a radio broadcast, a large and growing church, or possibly a well-known parachurch organization. Without these and other signs of success it is highly unlikely that anyone would give such a person the time of day.

But according to the Bible, success—genuine success—is the sovereign gift of God. When his jealous brothers sold Joseph into slavery and he was taken to Egypt, the Bible credits his ability to adapt and be successful to the sovereign work of God. It wasn't as simple as Joseph's pulling himself up by his own bootstraps. In the vernacular of today's success culture, someone might say that Joseph was handed a big lemon by his brothers and he made it into lemonade! But the reality is that it was God who was sovereignly at work behind the scenes in Joseph's life making him a success. In fact this was so obvious that even a pagan ruler could see that Joseph's success couldn't be attributed to his hard work and good attitude alone. In Genesis 39:2–3 we're told: "The LORD was with Joseph and blessed him greatly as he served in the home of his Egyptian master. *Potiphar noticed this and realized that the LORD was with Joseph, giving him success in everything he did.*"

In Proverbs God speaks through the wisdom writer:

> *Good advice and success belong to me.* Insight and strength are mine. Because of me, kings reign, and rulers make just laws. Rulers lead with my help, and nobles make righteous judgments. I love all who love me. Those who search for me will surely find me. *Unending riches, honor, wealth, and justice are mine to distribute.* My gifts are better than the purest gold, my wages better than sterling silver!
>
> Proverbs 8:14–19

These verses would seem to indicate that God is the source of success and gives it to whomever he desires for his sovereign purposes.

Though King Solomon certainly would qualify as a successful person by American cultural standards, we know from reading his own musings in the book of Ecclesiastes that he felt anything but successful despite his wealth, power, and influence.

In Ecclesiastes 4 Solomon, no doubt as the result of his own inner struggle to find true success, realizes that most people are motivated to gain the appearance and trappings of success for all of the wrong reasons, and that it is really no success at all. In verse 4 he states, "Then I observed that most people are motivated to success by their envy of their neighbors. But this, too, is meaningless, like chasing the wind."

Solomon realized that most of us tend to lust for the tangible measures of achievement as a result of our envy of others—we want what they have. So, motivated by our own dark side,[5] we obsessively work to acquire the

171

appearance of success, but at the end of the process, just like Solomon, when we have finally acquired the result we so desperately wanted, we discover we have nothing at all. We have been chasing the wind.

Clearly, the apostle Paul understood this as he shared with the Corinthians his perspective on noteworthy ministry. Paul saw the redeemed lives of the Corinthians as one of his greatest rewards. The eager reception of the gospel preached was one of his primary measures of success. In fact he tells the Corinthians that, "It is not that we think we can do anything of lasting value by ourselves. Our only power and success *come from God*" (2 Cor. 3:5).

When he possessed all of the outward markings of worldly accomplishment, Saul of Tarsus was an unmitigated failure in God's eyes. But when he let go of them all and began to follow God's sovereign plan for his life, he began to experience genuine fulfillment.

Once again, we must remember that genuine success can be experienced only as the sovereign gift of a loving God. We can amass mountains of earthly accoutrements that we hope will quantify our success for the world to see and yet still feel desperately insecure in what we have accomplished. Or we can begin to redefine the way we measure success and embark on the journey toward discovering one of the greatest treasures of all—serenity in God's sovereignty.

Seeking a Redefinition of Success

If we wish to redefine success, we must begin with God. What does God consider success to be? This will determine how we measure our personal and ministry success.

172

At some point on our ministry journey we have got to realize that we can build the biggest church in the world and actually see thousands of people coming to Christ, and still be an abysmal failure in the eyes of God. If our motives are impure, our methods dubious, and our personal character and spirituality seriously flawed, I do not believe God considers us successful. When people come to Christ through the ministry or work of such a ministry practitioner it speaks more of God's faithfulness to his Word than it does to that minister's success.

In my efforts to gain a new perspective on success, I have identified several qualitative indicators that seem to provide me with a more accurate measure of my current level of success than any possible combination of the more typical quantitative indicators we tend to use in ministry. Generally during my time of spiritual disciplines and especially during times of personal retreat, I assess how I am doing in these areas by asking myself a series of questions and then I journal my answers. By the time I am done, I have a pretty good idea if I am spiritually on track and viewing success as I should, or whether I may need to recenter my thinking. Maybe these questions will help you in your efforts to redefine the way you measure your personal and ministry success.

What Is the Current State of My Relationship with God?

One of the clear indicators that I am spiritually out of sync is when the state of my personal relationship with God is in decline or neutral. I am not suggesting that I fall in and out of relationship with God, but rather that there are times when the relationship loses its passion and intimacy. I still have my time of disciplines in

173

the morning but they are more perfunctory than they are personal and passionate. When I fall into one of these periods, it is usually because I have been attempting to give my life direction and am charging ahead under my own steam.

Another cause of my periodic spiritual staleness is the reality that I have been setting my heart and mind on the wrong things. After a period of setting my heart and mind on success from the world's perspective (for example, the need to get a new book deal, a bigger advance, more speaking opportunities, and the material benefits that these would provide), I find myself losing interest in eternal things. I really believe that is why the apostle John so strongly admonishes us:

> Stop loving this evil world and all that it offers you, for when you love the world, you show that you do not have the love of the Father in you. For the world offers only the lust for physical pleasure, the lust for everything we see, and pride in our possessions. These are not from the Father. They are from this evil world. And this world is fading away, along with everything it craves. But if you do the will of God, you will live forever.
>
> 1 John 2:15–17

That is exactly what happens to me when I begin to focus on what the world has to offer—I lose my love for the Father! Bombarded by the media as we are, and being constantly peppered by our culture's messages of success, it is a constant battle to keep from being sucked into the sweet but empty seduction to take charge of our life and grab our own "well-deserved" success. But falling in love with the world and all of the things it has to offer will mean falling out of love with God—we cannot love both God and the world.

Jesus said, "You must love the Lord your God with all your heart, all your soul, and all your mind" (Matt. 22:37). Our entire being is to be consumed with a love for God and a desire to love him still more. He is to occupy our deepest longings and desires. It is God whom we are encouraged to lust after. It is our sacred romance with the sovereign lover of our soul that will bring the serenity and satisfaction for which we long, a serenity and satisfaction that the world and its culture of success promise but can't deliver.[6]

If all I were able to do with the remainder of my life was to more consistently love God with all of my heart, soul, and mind, I could not achieve greater success. I pray that it will be so.

Am I Truly Enjoying My Ministry?

Another question that may reveal a wrong focus and help me redefine my view of success is asking simply whether or not I am genuinely enjoying my ministry.

For more than half of the years I have been in ministry, I have not truly enjoyed it. Many of those years were spent overwhelmed by stress and obsessed with church growth and tangible results because the ministry was more about me and advancing my goals and dreams for success than it was about loving God, sharing him with others, and advancing his kingdom.

Today, whenever I find myself stressed out in ministry and working way too many hours to achieve some goal or establish some program, it is probably because the goal is more important to me than it is to God—I need it more than he does.

I am convinced that true success can be measured by whether or not we are enjoying the ministry to which we have been called. That's not to say there are not dif-

175

ficult and painful experiences that are part of spiritual ministry. But even during the difficult times, when our focus is right, we can find serenity and contentment deep inside just as the apostle Paul did. In contrast, when we are consistently miserable and stressed out, it is a good indication that we have perverted our ministry into something God never intended it to be.

Joy and contentment in our calling, no matter how humble or grand, are true signs of success in ministry.

How Am I Treating People?

Without question, one of the sure signs that I have developed a perverted view of success is when I begin to use people as a means to *my* ends, rather than loving and motivating them to accomplish God's purposes.

Early in my ministry I struggled with the balance between motivation and manipulation in ministry. I suppose even then I was subtly aware of my inner cravings for success and significance, and was concerned that I not use the people of God to accomplish things that were really more about me than they were about God. I remember after a seminar I attended on stewardship and increasing the giving of your congregation, I approached the seminar presenter and asked, "What is the difference between motivation and manipulation?" The presenter, now a well-known, evangelical leadership authority, told me, "Manipulation involves attempting to move people in a direction for your own personal benefit, while motivation involves inspiring people to move in a direction for your mutual benefit as a congregation, in a way that will honor and glorify God." To this day I have remembered his words and am constantly monitoring whether I am motivating or manipulating.

176

My first executive minister always told me that a sure sign of my success in ministry would be when the people genuinely loved me and I genuinely loved them. Now, with nearly twenty years of experience and hindsight, I can't think of a better measure of true ministry success.

Don't get me wrong. I am in no way suggesting that we should strive in ministry to get people to like us. That is not what I am saying. When we love God with all of our heart, soul, and mind and are leading others into that same kind of relationship, there will be a deep bond of love between pastor and people. Even when we have to take an unpopular stand because it is the right thing to do or when we know we must lead the congregation in a direction that is not popular with many, when it honors God and benefits the people, they will ultimately sense it and that deep bond of love will remain.

How Am I Handling the Suffering That Is Part of Ministry?

Not long ago I received a scathing letter from one of my parishioners essentially outlining for me his top ten reasons why he didn't care for me or the way I was carrying out my ministry. To his credit he signed the letter, which is more than I can say for many with the gift of criticism. Unfortunately, most of the concerns in the letter were based on misinformation, rumors, and his personal preference for how ministry should be done. When I finished reading the letter, I could feel the anger creeping up my spine. *How dare he?* I thought indignantly. *What gives him the right to be so rude and mean?* It didn't help my response to know that he sleeps unapologetically through every service while I preach!

Immediately I was ready for battle. I'd put him in his place. I'd make sure he never did anything so rude and mean-spirited again! But even as I was working myself into a lather of self-righteous indignation, it was as if I could hear Jesus quietly choking out some of his final words on earth, "Father, forgive them. They don't know what they are doing." How could I become so angry as the result of a mindless letter written by a guy who sleeps through the service? What could possibly get me so riled up? The simple answer is that this episode revealed that my focus was on my image and me. I was incensed that anyone could think that way about *me* and be so mean to *me!*

However, I am beginning to understand that a true measure of genuine success is how I handle the suffering that is an inevitable part of ministry. When I can finally handle even the most unjust suffering with the grace and mercy Jesus showed, then I will know I am a true success.

The apostle Peter puts it this way:

> So then, since Christ suffered physical pain, you must arm yourselves with the same attitude he had, and be ready to suffer, too. For if you are willing to suffer for Christ, you have decided to stop sinning. *And you won't spend the rest of your life chasing after evil desires,* but you will be anxious to do the will of God. You have had enough in the past of the evil things that godless people enjoy—their immorality and lust, their feasting and drunkenness and wild parties, and their terrible worship of idols.
>
> 1 Peter 4:1–3

It is amazing to me that Peter equates our no longer chasing after the world's definition of success with how we handle suffering. You see, it's our willingness to suffer unjustly at the hands of mean and evil people that

178

shows we have begun measuring success from an eternal perspective.

Rather than becoming indignant and angry when we're called to endure unjust suffering at the hands of petty people, Peter says:

> Instead, be very glad [when you are called to suffer]—because these trials will make you partners with Christ in his suffering, and afterward you will have the wonderful joy of sharing his glory when it is displayed to all the world.

verse 13

Clearly Peter says that our willingness to welcome and endure suffering can be a sure sign that we are well on the path to true success. If you want to talk about experiencing real success, how about sharing with Jesus Christ in all his glory when it is displayed to the whole world. Now that's success!

We may never be seen on national television, speak to crowds of thousands, pastor the nation's largest church, or be a world-famous author. But if we are faithful now and have the proper view of success, the day is coming when we will be displayed with Christ for the whole world to see, when he is revealed in all his glory. God has the final word on what success truly looks like.

Other Indicators of Success to Monitor

Although these four indicators do not by any means provide a comprehensive and complete picture of what true success looks like from a biblical perspective, I believe they begin to get to the heart of the matter. Other indicators that I monitor on a regular basis include whether or not I am obediently following God in every

179

area of my life. This is closely tied to whatever the state of my relationship with God is like at any given time and is an important aspect to inventory regularly.

Another indicator that I am growing in a proper understanding of success is how well I am empowering others to spiritual progress and ministry effectiveness. A good sign for me is when I get more joy from the victories and triumphs of a staff member than I do from my own. When I find joy in the ministry triumphs of others, even when that means they receive greater recognition than I do, it is a sign that my redefinition of success is taking root in my heart.

There may be other signs that you can use to monitor the real success of your life. It is vital that they be more qualitative in nature than quantitative. Use them from time to time to assess whether you are spiritually on track.

In the final analysis we all long to hear from the Lord, "Well done, good and faithful servant." I am convinced that when we are consistently finding serenity in God's loving sovereignty and recklessly entrusting our life and ministry to him, there is no greater success. When we are finally able to let go of all the external measures that we have for so long equated with ministry success, and instead find our greatest joy and contentment in loving God with all of our heart, soul, and mind and experience a supernatural contentment regardless of the circumstance we face, we will be a success.

My prayer for you, as well as for myself, is that we may grow daily in our ability to find serenity in God's sovereignty as we seek to serve him with all of our being. God, may it be so. Amen.

Suggestions for Self-Reflection

1. How do you currently define success in your life and ministry?

2. How has your definition of success changed over time? What have been the precipitating factors in that change over the years?

3. Using a concordance, look up as many listings for *success* as you can. What seems to be a common theme in these texts? What implications does this have for your life and ministry?

4. At the present time would you say you measure success more in terms of the quantitative results produced by your efforts or by the quality of your experience with God, his people, and the ministry position to which he has called you? Give a reason for why you measure success in this way.

5. Take some time to journal your responses to the following questions:

   • What is the current state of my relationship with God?

   • Am I truly enjoying my ministry?

   • How am I treating the people I minister to and those who serve with me?

   • How am I handling the suffering that is an inevitable part of ministry?

   • How well am I empowering others for effective public ministry?

   • How much joy do I derive from the success of my ministry colleagues?

Conclusion

In chapter 4 of this book I made a confession of sorts. I confessed that I was struggling to find a measure of serenity and contentment in my own exercise of ministry. As I explained in chapter 3, as I was writing the first sections of this book, I was struggling with my sense of calling and was experiencing a deep longing to make a transition in ministry from that of a local church pastor to one more focused on the formation and development of leaders.

During that time of struggle I was tempted to believe that I could create a future for my life and ministry that would be fulfilling and would satisfy my longing. Because God wasn't moving as fast as I wanted him to, I considered giving God a little help and forcing the issue. In my spirit I knew that the way I was going about things was wrong and not the way God wanted to move me into a new ministry—but I was becoming impatient and frustrated with waiting for God to open the doors that I wanted to walk through.

Thankfully, with the help of a wise and discerning spiritual mentor, I realized that the timing for such a ministry transition was not right and the method purely human. God spoke clearly and said, "Wait." Through my time of reflection and spiritual direction the Lord clearly said, "Stay where you are and throw yourself back into the ministry of the local church to which I called you." There was no explanation or rationale offered, no promise of future fulfillment for my inner yearning, just a simple command to stay, wait, and recommit to the local church ministry to which I had been called.

So I made the decision to wait on God and I threw myself back into pastoral ministry with renewed commitment and a fresh excitement for what God wanted to do in my life and work. I was finally willing to acknowledge that God's plan for my life and ministry—whatever it might turn out to be—would be infinitely better than anything I could design on my own.

As a result of reflecting and journaling on the truths of Psalm 84:10–12, I arrived at the place where I could honestly say that I would rather spend one day in the place of God's choosing than one thousand days in the place of my own creation. I decided that one day as the pastor of any church, anywhere, if it was a church to which God had called me, would be better even than a ministry as a worldwide leadership teacher and author. I let go of my need to succeed according to my plans and schedule and allowed God to be in sovereign control of my life.

A Lesson on Success from the Sea

As twenty-first-century fishers of men, I am convinced that we all need to learn the lesson on success in ministry that Saint Peter learned from an encounter with Jesus, recorded in Luke 5:

184

When [Jesus] had finished speaking, he said to Simon, "Now go out where it is deeper and let down your nets, and you will catch many fish."

"Master," Simon replied, "we worked hard all last night and didn't catch a thing. But if you say so, we'll try again." And this time their nets were so full they began to tear! A shout for help brought their partners in the other boat, and soon both boats were filled with fish and on the verge of sinking. When Simon Peter realized what had happened, he fell to his knees before Jesus and said, "Oh, Lord, please leave me—I'm too much of a sinner to be around you." For he was awestruck by the size of their catch, as were the others with him. His partners, James and John, the sons of Zebedee, were also amazed.

Jesus replied to Simon, "Don't be afraid! From now on you'll be fishing for people!" And as soon as they landed, they left everything and followed Jesus.

Luke 5:4–11

No doubt most of us have heard more than one exposition of this passage. In fact most of us have probably even preached and taught it ourselves. But it is one of those stories with so many different layers of divine insight and truth that it is easy to skim past some of the simpler, more straightforward lessons.

One of the lessons I am convinced that Jesus is teaching here is the nature of success from an eternal perspective—what it looks like, where it comes from, and how it should impact our lives as Christ followers.

Obviously Peter and the others were skilled and experienced fishermen. They had fished that sea all of their lives and knew every cove and inlet. They knew well how to read the water and weather. They knew when the best time was to catch lots of fish. But in spite of their training, experience, and knowledge, they were unable to catch any fish on this particular occasion. I'm sure they were frustrated and confused by not catching a single fish when all of their fishing skills and intuition told them there should have been a bounty filling their boats by this time in the morning. But there was no bounty. They had been skunked and skunked good.

Then Jesus comes along and, it appears, rather non-chalantly says, "Now go out where it is deeper and let down your nets, and you will catch many fish." This was a carpenter telling seasoned fishermen where and how to catch fish—something akin to a truck-driving elder telling the seminary-trained pastor how to go about effective church growth and increase the size of the congregation. I'm sure you can imagine the natural and strong resistance to such unsolicited and unwelcome advice. But because it was Jesus, Simon Peter politely deferred and halfheartedly headed back onto the Sea of Galilee at a time of day when the sun was up high in the sky and any fisherman worth his salt would know that this was the worst of all possible times to catch fish.

Simple obedience to a command that made no professional sense was the difference between success and failure for Simon Peter and his fishing buddies. When they realized what had happened, they were humbled and awestruck at what Jesus had just done. Where they had previously failed after exhausting all of their know-how and effort, Jesus succeeded with just a word.

I am convinced that Simon spontaneously fell at the feet of Jesus in recognition of his divine, sovereign nature. Here was the one who was in control of the very fish in the sea. By virtue of his being the Creator of the universe, Jesus knew where every fish ever created was and he knew exactly what was needed to catch them at any given moment in time. No amount of human ingenuity, experience, skill, or effort could even begin to compete with the sovereign power of Jesus. For Peter, James, and John, success began that day with a profound recognition of and submission to the sovereignty of God.

Same Story, Different Sea

In a powerful sermon on this very text British pastor Percy C. Ainsworth made an astute application.

On the greater sea where you and I do our work the same story is told. It is difficult to understand, perhaps beyond us all. The failure of the foolish, the incompetent, and the lazy is a foregone conclusion. Yet often we see wise, strong, earnest, capable souls coming from their toils with nothing to show. It is wrong to account for the seeming lack of results by suggesting that the worker is incompetent. Some of the best-equipped lives the world has known have been associated with failure rather than success. For all of us, periods of unfruitful and unrewarded effort are only too familiar. For the fisherman in the bay, for the toiler among human souls, life holds something not fortuitous, but incalculable. There is always the unknown quantity. Always the equation we cannot solve. *It is not the will of God that we should consider ourselves masters of the work we have been given to do. It is enough to know God is the master of it.*[1]

Has your church and its lack of substantial growth become for you an unsolvable equation that has you perplexed and frustrated? Has the next step in your professional journey got you bewildered and stressed out? Do those stagnant or dwindling offerings represent for you that unknown quantity of which Ainsworth spoke? Let me ask you this: Have you yet begun to realize that it is not the will of God for you to be the master of *his* work that *he* has called you to do? Have you begun to grasp the cosmic reality that God is the absolute sovereign of all that we can comprehend? Are you now willing to recklessly entrust every aspect of your life and ministry into the competent hands of him who is the master of it all—the one who knows you and your dreams better than you do? Can you trust him, fully recognizing that he is the one who created you out of nothing and planted desires and dreams deep within your soul?

It is not until you are able to consistently rest in the sovereignty of God that you will begin to experience the serenity, joy, and eternal success in ministry for which your soul has been yearning.

Resting in the Sovereignty of God for the Catch of a Lifetime!

An amazing thing happened on the way to the conclusion of this book. Before I had finished the writing of it, God led me into the leadership ministry to which I had sensed he was calling me for some time. It is totally different, however, from what I would have planned for myself—it is much better and has provided some unanticipated blessings. Unexpectedly, God opened a door for me to become the District Executive Minister of the Columbia Baptist Conference. It is a position in which I have the privilege of serving the pastors and leaders of all the Baptist General Conference churches in the states of Alaska, Washington, Oregon, Idaho, and Montana. What an amazing opportunity to work with leaders! For the past twenty years my wife and I have dreamed of returning to minister in our home state of Washington, but God had never opened any doors for us to return home. It's amazing to us that the Columbia Baptist Conference is headquartered in Seattle, Washington—the very place we had wanted to move for at least the last ten years. And I have always dreamed of living on the water in the Pacific Northwest but never thought it would become a reality on a minister's income. But even in this small detail God blessed us beyond anything I could have ever planned or put together. He provided us with a house just one block from Puget Sound in the kind of area I have always dreamed of living in—not fancy, just a rustic, artistic little village by the sea.

Today, as I write these words in Alaska during a week-long stay where I am meeting with pastors and other leaders, I actually shudder to think of where I would be if I had followed my own plans.

During this most recent wrestling match between my plans and goals and the sovereign leadership of God in my life, God was saying to me, "Sam, I know the desires of your heart because I planted them there. I want you to realize your kingdom potential more than you ever could. But in order for that to happen, you are going to have to let go of your plans for life and ministry and recklessly trust me with everything."

God was simply telling me to go back to the sea in which I had been fishing, back to the local ministry where he had placed me. Though I hadn't yet seen the type of catch I was looking for at that place, God knew what he was doing. And, with the help of a wise spiritual mentor and much prayer and reflection, I was willing to go back to the deeper water where God was preparing to fill my boat to overflowing.

Finding Serenity and Success in the Sovereignty of God

So go on. Go back out to the deeper water. Go with your fear and your uncertainty and your inability to connect all of the dots for a perfect future. But go with the

189

unshakable faith that he who sent you is the master of all there is to master. Let go of your life and recklessly entrust it to God, knowing beyond all doubt that he will make far more of it than you ever could on even your best day. Learn to listen daily, moment by moment, to hear his voice and obey, understanding beyond all doubt that he knows what success looks like for you. It is then, and only then, that you and I will find serenity in God's sovereignty and experience a renewed measure of joy and contentment in life and ministry regardless of what it looks like from a human perspective.

May we each begin to increasingly experience the serenity and significance for which our souls yearn as we learn to daily rest in the sovereignty of God. Lord, let it be so, we pray! Amen.

$\mathcal{N}otes$

Chapter 2 Recipes for Success

1. Gene Appel and Alan Nelson, *How to Change Your Church without Killing It* (Nashville: Word Publishing, 2000), 10, 15.

Chapter 3 Personal Ministry Success versus God's Sovereignty

1. See Jeff Imbach, *The River Within: Loving God, Living Passionately* (Colorado Springs: NavPress, 1998).

Chapter 4 Success Sickness

1. Mark Mittleberg, *Building a Contagious Church: Revolutionizing the Way We View and Do Evangelism* (Grand Rapids: Zondervan, 2000).

2. Appel and Nelson, *How to Change Your Church without Killing It,* 15.

3. Percy C. Ainsworth, "The Miraculous Draught of Fishes," *Weavings* 16, no. 2 (March/April 2001): 29.

4. *The Mitchell Report,* Friday, November 10, 2000, on MSNBC.

5. See David Maraniss and Ellen Nakashima, *The Prince of Tennessee* (New York: Simon and Schuster, 2000).

6. *NBC Nightly News,* Friday, November 10, 2000.

7. *Nightline,* Friday, November 10, 2000, on ABC.

Chapter 5 Letting Go of the Need to Succeed

1. J. Robert Clinton, *The Making of a Leader* (Colorado Springs: NavPress, 1988), 238.

2. This passage, as well as the Ephesians 2:10 passage, will be discussed in greater detail in chapter 6.

3. For more information on the Leadership Central Program, go to www.LeadershipCentral.org or www.visionnw.org.

4. Brennan Manning, *Ruthless Trust* (San Francisco: HarperSanFrancisco, 2000), 177.

Chapter 6 Our Stimulus to Trust

1. Manning, *Ruthless Trust*, 9.
2. Millard Erickson, *Christian Theology* (Grand Rapids: Baker, 1985), 400.
3. Ibid.
4. Ibid.
5. Brenton Brown, "Lord, Reign in Me," © 1998 Vineyard Songs (UK/EIRE). Administered by Mercy/Vineyard Publishing in North America (ASCAP). All rights reserved. Used by permission.

Chapter 7 God's Loving Sovereignty

1. Robert Spector, *Amazon.Com: Get Big Fast* (San Francisco: HarperBusiness, 2000), 234.
2. Ibid., 230.

Chapter 8 Redefining Ministry Success in Light of God's Loving Sovereignty

1. Ken Blanchard, "Gung-ho for God," *Life@Work Journal,* Leadership Summit Edition (August 2000), 18.
2. Ibid.
3. Kent Hughes, "Feelings of Failure," *Leadership* (spring 1987), 27.
4. *USA Today* (January 22, 2001), sec. D, p. 1.
5. See Gary L. McIntosh and Samuel D. Rima Sr., *Overcoming the Dark Side of Leadership: The Paradox of Personal Dysfunction* (Grand Rapids: Baker, 1997), 22.
6. Let me encourage you to read *The Sacred Romance: Drawing Closer to the Heart of God* by Brent Curtis and John Eldridge (Nashville: Thomas Nelson, 1997), as a way to whet your appetite for a deeper, more intimate love relationship with the Father.

Conclusion

1. Ainsworth, "Miraculous Draught of Fishes," 27. Emphasis mine.